Praise for *Cooking Is Cool*

"I can't tell you how excited I am that somebody finally made a cookbook that lets children actually prepare the food themselves. Children love to cook, and I am thrilled to be using *Cooking Is Cool* at our center!"

—**Julie McCollumn, owner and director, Kids Club Child Care Center**

"An exciting book with a great variety of cooking activities that engage children."

—**Colleen Moynihan, owner, Pea Pods Child Care Center**

"We love this book! I have two daughters, ages four and six, who are always eager to help in the kitchen. We have had so much fun trying the recipes; the book suggestions add another element of fun. I highly recommend this book to anyone who wants to help introduce cooking to kids!"

—**Megan Vargulick, parent**

"This book is unique in its incredible ability to create perfect bonding experiences between children and adults. Any parent or educator would feel lucky to own this fun and brilliant work!"

—**Ashleigh Voros, parent and education major at the State University of New York (SUNY) at Geneseo**

"We love the book and have tried all the recipes. Not only do they taste delicious, but they are easy and fun for the kids to make! The kids ask me all the time to make the Fairy Tale Punch."

—**Bianca Affronti, preschool teacher, Pea Pods Child Care Center**

"It's not always possible to use an oven in a child care setting, but with this book I can make healthy, fun, and easy snacks all the time. I have tried some of the recipes with my kids, and they loved making them and then eating what they made. This book provides great ways to spend time with kids."

—**Brooke Nicholson, prekindergarten teacher**

COOKING
IS COOL

Heat-Free Recipes for Kids to Cook

Marianne E. Dambra

Redleaf Press®
www.redleafpress.org
800-423-8309

Published by Redleaf Press
10 Yorkton Court
St. Paul, MN 55117
www.redleafpress.org

First edition 2013
Cover design by Jim Handrigan
Cover photograph © Blend Images Photography/Veer
Interior design by Percolator
Typeset in Chaparral, Myriad, and Mrs. Eaves
Interior photographs by Jeff Lange except on page iii, by Brie Dambra, and pages 2 and 3,
    by Marianne E. Dambra
Printed in the United States of America
20 19 18 17 16 15 14 13   1 2 3 4 5 6 7 8

Library of Congress Cataloging-in-Publication Data
Dambra, Marianne E.
  Cooking is cool: heat-free recipes for kids to cook / Marianne E. Dambra. — First edition.
      pages cm
   Includes index.
   Summary: "Help children experience the many benefits and joys of cooking—all without entering the kitchen or using the stove or oven. Heat-free, classroom-friendly recipes are included, each designed so that children can help prepare healthy appetizers and dips, beverages, snacks and treats, and sandwiches and salads as they explore new foods, build math and literacy skills, and learn about nutrition." — Provided by publisher.
    ISBN 978-1-60554-158-7 (pbk.)
    ISBN 978-1-60554-258-4 (e-book)
    1. Cold dishes (Cooking)—Juvenile literature.   I. Title.
  TX830.D36 2013
  641.7'9—dc23
                          2013003779

Printed on acid-free paper

In memory of a wonderful friend, classroom coteacher, and cooking fool,
Jim Hoey, who was taken away far too early.

CONTENTS

ACKNOWLEDGMENTS

I would like to thank MaryAnn Kohl, my agent, my friend, and the person who encouraged me for ten years to write this book. Without her enthusiasm, help, creativity, and support, this book would not have happened. Thanks to Sue Inzero for her primary edit of this book. Her keen eye helped make this dream possible. For the beautiful photographs, special thanks to Jeff Lange. Without his flexibility and creativity, even with butter, the photographs would not have happened. Thank you to all the people at Redleaf Press, especially David Heath, my editor, for his patience and continued support. Special thanks to my cousins and friends who spent extra time helping with the photography. I am ever so grateful to Kids Club Child Care Center in Avon, New York; Pea Pods Child Care Center in Penfield, New York; and Generations Early Care and Education Centers in Rochester, New York, for allowing me to share my recipes with the children and teachers. Most important, thanks to my husband, Sam; my daughter, Brie; my parents, Anthony and Mary Anne; and my brother, Anthony. Their support was never ending!

INTRODUCTION: LEARNING THROUGH COOKING

Children love to cook! Cooking is an activity that most children, both boys and girls, enjoy. Countless important teachable moments take place while cooking. When we think of the importance of pretend play, where children imitate and explore what they know, we see that cooking extends their play and invites them to step beyond just play, and to cook with real ingredients and supplies, not just props. Children will plan what to cook, gather the equipment, prepare the ingredients, talk about what they think may happen, and evaluate the outcome. Providing these firsthand and well-planned experiences is an important part of the early childhood curriculum.

What Learning Takes Place?

Language plays a large role in the cooking experience. Starting with reading recipes, children learn that we read from left to right. They develop the skills to follow written and verbal instructions. Children will ask questions about the processes, predict what may come next, and talk about the outcome. Pre-reading skills develop, such as associating words with ingredients.

New vocabulary is plentiful. Children will discuss the variety of foods in their world, some familiar and some new. They will explore new experiences with equipment from blenders to whisks. Young cooks will discover and implement cooking techniques, such as mashing and dicing. Beginning writing skills are developed when children are given opportunities to write, dictate, and illustrate recipes that have been completed. Each recipe has a suggested story-book that can be incorporated into the cooking learning experience.

Math skills are an important part of cooking! Children will learn simple arithmetic through measurements that include whole numbers and fractions, counting and sorting the number of ingredients needed, and learning about one-to-one correspondences. Classification is explored when categorizing ingredients such as wet or dry, fruit or vegetable, hard or soft. Children learn sequencing as they follow the steps for each recipe and count out loud to reinforce these abilities. All these skills are important concepts of mathematics.

Cooking science seems like magic to beginning cooks. Children are given an opportunity to experiment, ask questions, make predictions, and test those predictions. They will see the changes in matter, from liquid to solid, solid to liquid, and changes in color and texture. You can extend their knowledge of where foods come from by planting seeds in soil and studying the outcome. Consider investigating the different origins of foods included in the recipes.

When the children prepare recipes, they develop their small- and large-motor skills and learn kinesthetically from touch. When they are cutting, chopping, and turning the pages of recipe books, children are developing their small-motor skills. When they are mixing, folding, and rolling out ingredients, they are developing large-motor skills.

As children learn to take turns and share, they are developing their social and emotional skills. Children feel a sense of pride when they have completed a recipe. Cooking in small groups allows for children to take turns, develop independence, understand cooperation, and become aware of and respect others.

Of course cooking entails nutrition, an important part of cooking and learning for children. All children are encouraged to try new foods, create healthy snacks and meals, and learn about food groups. Learning about the importance of exercise and being healthy is a significant part of cooking experiences.

Getting Started

"I can't cook with my children because I don't have a kitchen!" I often hear these exact words from many educators, teachers, parents, and child care providers. Would you believe you don't need a kitchen to cook in your classroom or even in your home? With the encouragement of a colleague, I created a "Kitchen on Wheels" using an old water play table that had a top to work on with space underneath and inside for supplies.

The portable table became a multipurpose learning center in my classroom. It was a center for cooking activities to do with a group as well as individually. I kept basic playdough supplies available so the children were able to make playdough as needed. Of course the children needed supervision, but it did not require me to be next to them during the entire process. The problem-solving exchanges were delightful to observe.

In the afternoons, it became our snack center. Children were able to help themselves to a snack when they were ready. There were picture recipe cards showing the children how much of each item they could take to start with. Stopping play to eat snack was no longer necessary; it was there for them when they were ready. Children playing as a group would clean up and go to the snack area together. I loved it, and they loved it! The children had the independence to eat when they were ready.

Getting supplies was easier than I imagined. I sent out invitations to the parents for a "Kitchen Shower" listing the basic equipment we would need for cooking, such as mixing bowls and mixing spoons, and the parents provided them. Most items can be found at dollar stores, so the cost is reduced! I also kept basic staples on hand such as flour, salt, sugar, and food coloring.

No longer did I need to bring my kitchen from home to cook with my class! The cooking center was our kitchen!

Cooking with Ease: Tips and Safety

Here are some ideas that will help make your cooking activities safe and successful.

Before You Begin

- Read the whole recipe before you start cooking.
- Gather all your foods and equipment before you start cooking. Organization is the secret to successful cooking experiences.
- Include the children in everything—setup, cooking, cleanup, etc.
- Demonstrate and explain how to use the equipment before you begin.
- Clean up spills as they occur. This will prevent accidents that might happen due to spills on the floor.

Staying Healthy

- Always wash your hands when you begin cooking and anytime they become soiled. When washing your hands, make sure to use warm water and rub your hands together for twenty seconds.
- Wash all fruits and vegetables before using them in the recipes.
- Keep in mind any allergies children may have. Peanut warning: An increasing number of children are allergic to nuts and nut products. A nut or peanut allergy can cause difficulty breathing and other serious health problems. Warnings about nuts are listed in each recipe as needed. Substitute ingredients when nut allergies are a concern.

Keeping Safe

- Always have a first aid kit in the classroom (one should be available in every classroom, learning center, and home).
- Always consider a child's physical developmental level before allowing him or her to use any equipment, especially equipment that has potential dangers.
- Use proper supervision when using sharp utensils. Help children understand the need to cut away from themselves and others.
- When opening canned goods, be careful of the sharp edges on the lid.
- Permit only adults to remove food from the blender.
- Turn off and unplug each appliance immediately after use. Keep appliance cords tidy and out of children's reach.
- Remember to store foods properly as listed in the recipe.

And Finally . . .

- Don't worry about the end product.
- Do less so that the children do more.
- Remember that the rewards will outnumber the hassles.
- Separate children into small groups whenever possible.
- Have fun!

Cooking without a Kitchen: Equipment List

- measuring cups and spoons
- small, medium, and large bowls for mixing
- mixing spoon (wooden or plastic)
- spoons, forks, sharp knives, and table knives
- rubber spatula
- whisk
- aluminum foil, plastic wrap, and wax paper
- plastic ziplock storage bags, gallon and quart size
- plastic ziplock freezer bags, gallon and quart size
- can opener
- blender
- paper cups and clear plastic cups

- craft sticks
- cutting board
- serving plates
- 9-by-13-inch cake pan
- electric hand mixer
- rolling pin
- cookie sheet
- hand grater
- small, medium, and large food storage containers with lids
- optional: apple corer, toothpicks

Chapter 1
APPETIZERS AND DIPS

· · · · · · · · · · · · · · · · · · · ·

· · · · · · · · · · · · · · · · · · · ·

Appetizers and dips are usually served before a meal or as a snack. They are served to stimulate the appetite.

The appetizers provided in this chapter include recipes that are perfect for beginning cooks. The recipes are organized to provide simple recipes first, such as butter, and then more-complex recipes later, such as salsa. It is a good idea to start cooking foods that are familiar to children first, such as butter and whipped cream.

Keep in mind the importance of encouraging children to use their senses as they cook. Let children use an electric hand mixer to feel the vibration and hear the blades mixing the food. Invite the children to observe changes that occur during the cooking process. And of course everyone will enjoy the aroma of the food!

As they make these recipes, the children will enjoy their firsthand experiences while cooking. Getting the children involved allows us to use the teachable moments to reinforce many of the skills they are already learning. Take the time to write down what children are saying as they cook. Their thoughts and insights can be used to enhance your curriculum.

Did You Know?

Butter has been artificially colored yellow since the fourteenth century. Marigolds, which are bright orange flowers, were once used to color butter.

HOMEMADE BUTTER

Making butter is the ideal recipe for introducing beginning cooks to following the steps in a recipe. Butter is easily made with heavy whipping cream and salt.

Ingredients

1 cup heavy whipping cream
Salt to taste
Crackers or bread for serving

Equipment

Mixing bowl, chilled
Electric hand mixer
Table knife
Plates for serving
Medium food storage container
    with lid

Directions

1 Place the heavy whipping cream in chilled mixing bowl.

2 Using an electric mixer, mix cream on high speed.

3 The cream will go from a liquid, to a soft cream, to a hard cream.

4 Once it has become a hard cream, the butter is done.

5 Add salt for desired taste.

6 Spread onto crackers or bread.

7 Store remaining butter in the refrigerator in a food storage container with lid.

Extension

What color is the butter you made?

A Book to Read

Like Butter on Pancakes by Jonathan London is a wonderful story about a young farm boy's day as the sun rises and the sun sets.

Yield: Makes 96 servings. Serving size 1 teaspoon.
Nutritional information for butter: 2 grams fat, 0 grams carbohydrates, 0 grams fiber, 0 grams protein.

Did You Know?

There is a sign over the door at Winnie-the-Pooh's house that says "Mr. Sanders." This name belongs to the person who lived at the address before Winnie-the-Pooh made it his house.

POOH BUTTER

Butter sweetened with honey is perfect for any bear. Make some extra Pooh Butter on January 18, National Winnie–the–Pooh Day!

Ingredients

1 tablespoon honey
1 tablespoon butter, softened
    (see homemade butter recipe
    on page 9)
Graham crackers for serving

Equipment

Mixing bowl
Mixing spoon
Measuring spoons
Table knife
Plates for serving

Directions

1 Mix equal parts of honey and butter. Begin with 1 tablespoon of each, adding a little more if necessary.

2 Stir until completely blended.

3 Spread blended mixture on graham crackers.

Extension

Do you like honey? Why do you think bears like honey?

A Book to Read

Winnie-the-Pooh: The Honey Tree by A. A. Milne is a story about Winnie-the-Pooh's adventure as he tries to learn why bees make their honey up high in a tree.

Yield: Makes 6 servings. Serving size 1 teaspoon.
Nutritional information for butter: 0.5 grams fat, 3 grams carbohydrates, 0 grams fiber, 0 grams protein.

Did You Know?

Whipped cream originated in France. In the
United States, National Whipped Cream Day
is celebrated each year on January 5.

WHIPPED CREAM

Whipped cream is a tasty addition for several recipes included in this book. This recipe starts out as liquid and becomes a soft cream in a matter of minutes.

Ingredients

1 cup heavy whipping cream

Equipment

Large mixing bowl, chilled
Electric hand mixer
Rubber spatula

Directions

1 Chill mixing bowl before you begin.

2 Pour heavy whipping cream into a chilled mixing bowl.

3 Using an electric hand mixer, begin mixing the cream on high.

4 The cream will begin to become thicker. When it reaches the consistency of a stiff peak, you have made your whipped cream.

Extension

Try freezing whipped cream! Place dollops of whipped cream on a cookie sheet covered with parchment paper and freeze. What do you think will happen?

A Book to Read

Big Brown Rooster and his friends Turtle, Iguana, and Potbellied Pig want to make a strawberry shortcake, but no one knows how to cook! Find out if the animals can learn to cook in *Cook-a-Doodle-Doo!* by Janet Stevens and Susan Stevens Crummel.

Yield: Makes 96 servings. Serving size 1 teaspoon.

Nutritional information for whipped cream: 1 gram fat, 0 grams carbohydrates, 0 grams fiber, 0 grams protein.

Did You Know?

Bees use their legs to transform the honey-comb into a hexagon (six-sided) shape.

HONEY-YOGURT DIP

This creamy dip adds just enough sweetness to bring out the variety of tastes in the fruits. Include this recipe in your September plans, for September is National Honey Month.

Ingredients

2 cups vanilla yogurt

½ cup honey

1 teaspoon ground cinnamon

Fresh fruits, such as apples, bananas, and strawberries, for dipping

Equipment

Mixing bowl

Mixing spoon

Measuring cups

Measuring spoons

Cutting board

Sharp knife

Spoon

Small bowls for serving

Plates for serving

Directions

1 Combine yogurt, honey, and ground cinnamon in a mixing bowl.

2 Stir until ingredients are blended.

3 Spoon into small bowls for dipping.

4 Cut fresh fruit, such as apples, bananas, and strawberries, into bite-size pieces and serve.

Extension

Try varying the yogurt flavors in the dip. Make a chart showing how many of the children liked which flavors or which was their favorite flavor.

A Book to Read

The Honeybee and the Robber by Eric Carle is a playful story about a honeybee and her adventure to get some nectar.

Yield: Makes 20 servings. Serving size 2 tablespoons.

Nutritional information for dip: 0 grams fat, 10 grams carbohydrates, 0 grams fiber, 1 gram protein.

Did You Know?

- Pumpkins are 90 percent water.
- Pumpkins are a fruit because they flower and have seeds.
- Pumpkins come in many shapes and sizes.
- Pumpkin colors can be yellow, white, green, tan, red, and even blue.

FLUFFY PUMPKIN DIP

Children can make a fluffy dip that is great for a crisp autumn day. This recipe offers children a firsthand taste of lightly sweetened pumpkin mixed with spices, milk, and sugar.

Ingredients

1 8-ounce container vanilla yogurt
1 15-ounce can solid packed pumpkin
¼ cup brown sugar
½ teaspoon ground cinnamon
¼ teaspoon ground ginger
⅛ teaspoon ground allspice
⅛ teaspoon ground nutmeg
2 cups whipped cream (see whipped
   cream recipe on page 13)
Cinnamon or regular graham crackers,
   gingersnap cookies, and cut fruit
   for dipping

Equipment

Mixing bowl
Mixing spoon
Measuring cups
Measuring spoons
Whisk
Plastic wrap

Directions

1 In a mixing bowl add yogurt, pumpkin, brown sugar, cinnamon, ginger, allspice, and nutmeg. Whip with a whisk until mixed thoroughly.

2 Fold in whipped cream until combined.

3 Cover the bowl with plastic wrap and chill for two hours.

4 Serve as a dip with cinnamon or regular graham crackers, gingersnap cookies, and cut fruit.

Extension
What color are pumpkins? Seek out pumpkins in a variety of colors and shapes for discussion.

A Book to Read
It's Pumpkin Time! by Zoe Hall tells the story of a brother and sister and the pumpkin seed they plant.

Yield: Makes 40 servings. Serving size 2 tablespoons.
Nutritional information for dip: 2 grams fat, 3 grams carbohydrates, 0 gram fiber, 1 gram protein.

Did You Know?

Making an alternative to cream cheese is quite simple using only one ingredient—yogurt. Line a colander with layers of fine cheesecloth, pour in 1 quart of yogurt, cover, and let drain into a bowl for at least five hours in the refrigerator. You've made yogurt cheese!

FLUFFY CREAM CHEESE FRUIT DIP

This dip is fluffy like a cloud! It's a creamy addition to fruit bites. Try using flavored cream cheese as an alternative to plain cream cheese. Celebrate National Fresh Fruit and Vegetables Month in June with this recipe.

Ingredients

8 ounces cream cheese, softened

¼ cup honey

1 tablespoon lemon juice

1 teaspoon pure vanilla extract

Fresh fruit cut into wedges or bite-size
   pieces for dipping

Equipment

Mixing spoon

Measuring cups

Measuring spoons

Mixing bowl

Serving bowl

Sharp knife

Cutting board

Small plates for serving

Directions

1 Mix cream cheese with honey, lemon juice, and vanilla extract until well blended.

2 Put mixture into a serving bowl.

3 Cut fruit into bite-size pieces.

4 Serve dip with fruit.

Extension

What fruits are your favorites to eat with fluffy cream cheese fruit dip? Use a graph or language chart to list the results.

A Book to Read

In *Fluffy and Baron* by Laura Rankin there is a beautiful friendship between Baron, a German shepherd dog, and a duckling named Fluffy. Find out what happens when Fluffy goes to the pond.

Yield: Makes 10 servings. Serving size 2 tablespoons.

Nutritional information for dip: 8 grams fat, 8 grams carbohydrates, 0 grams fiber, 1 gram protein.

Did You Know?

- In Mexico, tacos are as popular as sandwiches are in the United States.

- The word *taco* means "small or light snack."

TACO DIP

Quick and easy to make, this layered dip provides a great opportunity for talking about different vegetables, their colors, and how many layers they make together.

Ingredients

Shredded lettuce

1 diced tomato

8 ounces sour cream

8 ounces softened cream cheese

1 1½-ounce envelope of taco
    seasoning

1 cup shredded cheddar cheese

½ cup sliced black olives (optional)

Tortilla chips for dipping

Equipment

Measuring cup

Mixing bowl

Mixing spoon

Hand grater

Sharp knife

Cutting board

Electric hand mixer (optional)

9-by-13-inch pan

Serving bowl

Small plates for serving

Directions

1 Using a sharp knife, shred lettuce and set it aside.

2 Dice tomatoes into small cubes; set them aside.

3 Mix sour cream, softened cream cheese, and taco seasoning until well blended. (Use an electric hand mixer on high speed if you like.)

4 Spread mixture into a 9-by-13-inch pan.

5 Layer shredded lettuce over seasoned mixture.

6 Layer diced tomatoes over lettuce.

7 Sprinkle cheddar cheese over tomatoes.

8 Top off the layers with sliced black olives.

9 Serve dip with tortilla chips.

Extension

Show the children what a corn tortilla looks like before it is baked and packaged. What differences or similarities do children observe between an uncooked tortilla and one that has been cooked?

A Book to Read

Read about Mario and his sister Marissa's special taco in *Mud Tacos* by Mario Lopez and Marissa Lopez Wong.

Yield: Makes 15 servings. Serving size 4 tablespoons.

Nutritional information for dip: 11 grams fat, 4 grams carbohydrates, 1 gram fiber, 3 grams protein.

Did You Know?

Salsa (SAL-sah) is a Spanish word for sauce. Salsa is believed to have originated with the Inca people in what is now Peru. The Aztec and Mayan people also made salsa from tomatoes, chili peppers, and ground squash seeds. Salsa was given its name in 1571 by Alonso de Molino.

SALSA

Salsa is a Mexican tomato mixture for dipping tortilla chips. Try it with a variety of differently flavored tortilla chips.

Ingredients

1½ cups diced tomatoes
½ cup diced green peppers
½ cup chopped scallions (green onions)
1 tablespoon minced garlic
1 tablespoon cider vinegar
1 tablespoon olive oil
1 teaspoon oregano
1 teaspoon parsley
1 teaspoon salt
Tortilla chips for dipping

Equipment

Measuring cups
Measuring spoons
Mixing bowl
Mixing spoon
Sharp knife
Cutting board
Small bowls for serving

Directions

1 With adult supervision, use a sharp knife and cutting board to dice tomatoes and green peppers into very small cube shapes. (Warning: Have children wash their hands after handling peppers; and make sure they avoid touching their faces until they do so.)

2 Chop the scallions, measure, and then mix with the tomatoes and green peppers.

3 Combine garlic, vinegar, olive oil, oregano, and parsley in a mixing bowl. Add the chopped vegetables to the bowl and mix well. Add salt to taste if desired.

4 Refrigerate before serving. (Hint: The longer the salsa is chilled, the more the vegetable flavors will blend and the juicier it will become.)

5 Serve with tortilla chips.

6 Refrigerate leftovers for another tasty snack.

Extension
Sweet peppers come in a variety of different colors. Do a taste test of each colored pepper. Chart the responses or favorites.

A Book to Read
Mi Casa/My House by George Ancona is a sweet story about Araceli, a young girl from Mexico. Araceli tells her story about living on a ranch in Oregon.

Yield: Makes 20 servings. Serving size 2 tablespoons.
Nutritional information for salsa: 1 gram fat, 1 gram carbohydrate, 0 grams fiber, 0 grams protein.

BEVERAGES

· ·

· ·

Beverages can be wonderful, healthy refreshments. Nutritious ingredients such as yogurt, milk, and 100 percent fruit juice should always be used. Some of the recipes in this chapter introduce flavors that may be new to children, such as Concord grape juice, coconut milk, and unsweetened cocoa powder. Children can be shown the proper ways to use a blender and the importance of safety in using it.

As you go through the recipes, take the time to enhance language skills. Let the children read through the recipes with you, step by step, to show the importance of following directions. Encourage science inquiry by having children predict what changes will occur as they follow the recipe. Children will learn math concepts such as weights and fractions.

The US Department of Agriculture's Child and Adult Care Food Program (CACFP) suggests that children ages three through five years old receive a half-cup serving for snacktime. All the recipes in this chapter are designed for this suggestion.

Did You Know?

Bananas do not grow on trees. The banana plant, which can reach thirty feet high in a single year, does not have a woody trunk. The plant is really the world's largest herb!

BANANA CREAM PIE SMOOTHIE

This beverage is a smooth combination of bananas and yogurt topped off with graham cracker crumbs. Serve with Monkey Meals, page 63.

Ingredients

1 banana
1 cup vanilla yogurt
½ cup 2 percent milk
1 tablespoon nonfat dry milk
½ teaspoon pure vanilla extract
2 tablespoons graham cracker crumbs
1 cup crushed ice cubes
Additional graham cracker crumbs
    for topping

Equipment

Blender
Measuring cups
Measuring spoons
Sharp knife
Cutting board
Spoon
Cups for serving

Directions

1 Cut bananas into bite-size pieces. Place banana pieces in the blender and blend on high speed for ten seconds. Shut off blender.

2 Add yogurt, milk, dry milk, pure vanilla extract, and graham crackers, and blend well. Shut off blender.

3 Add ice cubes and blend again until the mixture is smooth. Shut off blender.

4 Pour into cups and sprinkle the top of each smoothie with graham cracker crumbs.

Extension

How does dry milk taste compared to 2 percent milk? Use the directions on the box to make the dry milk into a liquid. Make a chart to compare the tastes.

A Book to Read

In *Banana!* by Ed Vere, two monkeys attempting to share a banana try to stay out of trouble!

Yield: Makes 5 servings. Serving size ½ cup.
Nutritional information for smoothie: 1 gram fat, 16 grams carbohydrates, 1 gram fiber, 4 grams protein.

Did You Know?

Bananas peels have medicinal uses. Try rubbing the inside of a banana peel on a mosquito bite and see how it helps eliminate the itch.

COCOA BANANA SHAKE

Cocoa powder blended with a ripe banana and milk results in a delicious milk shake children can make in a blender.

Ingredients

2 cups 2 percent milk
4 tablespoons unsweetened
    cocoa powder
2 ripe bananas

Equipment

Blender
Measuring cups
Measuring spoons
Sharp knife
Cutting board
Cups for serving

Directions

1 Place milk and cocoa powder in blender.

2 Mix on high for ten seconds. Shut off blender.

3 Cut banana into bite-size pieces and place in blender.

4 Blend for ten seconds until smooth. Shut off blender.

5 Pour into cups to drink.

Extension

Does unsweetened cocoa taste different from sweetened cocoa? What differences can you find?

A Book to Read

In *The Boy Who Loved Bananas* by George Elliott, Matthew refuses to eat anything but bananas. Read about Matthew's banana-eating binge and learn what happens next!

Yield: Makes 4 servings. Serving size ½ cup.
Nutritional information for shake: 3 grams fat, 23 grams carbohydrates, 3 grams fiber, 7 grams protein.

FAIRY TALE PUNCH

This healthy drink includes lots of fresh fruit that children can blend with juice. It is perfect for sipping during or after story time.

Ingredients

1 cup diced apples

1 cup diced peaches

1 cup strawberries

1 diced banana

3 cups fresh fruit juice or bottled
   100 percent fruit juice (any flavor)

1 cup crushed ice cubes

Equipment

Blender

Measuring cups

Sharp knife

Cutting board

Cups for serving

Apple corer (optional)

Directions

1 Cut fruit and place in blender.

2 Add juice to blender and mix on high speed until smooth. Shut off blender.

3 Serve immediately with ice cubes, or freeze for an hour to make a slushy.

Extension

Talk about fairy tales that can't be seen at the movies. Storytelling is an art that children can enjoy by listening and acting out. Consider reading and acting out "Little Red Riding Hood," "The Three Billy Goats Gruff," or "The Princess and the Pea."

A Book to Read

A First Book of Fairy Tales by Mary Hoffman is a great storybook that introduces children to fairy tales, including "Cinderella," "Jack and the Beanstalk," "The Frog Prince," "Rumpelstiltskin," and other favorites.

Yield: Makes 10 servings. Serving size ½ cup.

Nutritional information for punch: 0 grams fat, 14 grams carbohydrates, 1 gram fiber, 0 grams protein.

Did You Know?

The key lime is a smaller variety of limes. A Persian variety is called Bearss and is seedless.

LEMON–LIME BUBBLY

This combination of fresh lemon juice, fresh lime juice, and apple juice becomes a delicious bubbly drink when mixed with soda water.

Ingredients

2 tablespoons fresh lemon juice

1 tablespoon fresh lime juice

1 cup soda water

1 cup + 2 tablespoons thawed apple juice concentrate

4 ice cubes

Equipment

Blender

Measuring cups

Measuring spoons

Cups for serving

Directions

1 Squeeze juice from lemons and limes; measure accordingly. (Hint: To get the maximum juice from a lemon or a lime, before juicing it make sure the fruit is at room temperature, and then roll it around on a countertop with the heel of your hand until it softens.)

2 Add lemon and lime juices, soda water, and apple juice concentrate to blender, and blend well on high speed for ten seconds. Shut off blender.

3 Serve in cups with an ice cube.

Extension

Bubble Prints

- Fill about ⅓ of an 8-ounce cup with water. Then add 2 tablespoons of tempera paint and 1 teaspoon of liquid dish-washing soap.
- Place the cup on a sheet of white construction paper.
- Have a child place a straw in the water and blow into the straw. Let the bubbles overflow onto the construction paper. As the bubbles overflow, they leave prints on the paper.

A Book to Read

In *Bubble Trouble* by Margaret Mahy, Mabel blows a bubble so big that it engulfs her baby brother and carries him away. Children will enjoy all the silly adventures that follow.

Yield: Makes 4 servings. Serving size ½ cup.

Nutritional information for drink: 0 grams fat, 18 grams carbohydrates, 0 grams fiber, 0 grams protein.

Did You Know?

Peaches came from China, where they have been grown for over three thousand years. In Chinese culture, the peach is a symbol of long life. Chinese brides carry peach blossoms at their weddings.

PEACHY BANANA DRINK

All fruit drinks can be tasty, but this combination of bananas and peaches is a favorite. Drink it from a cup, or eat it with a spoon.

Ingredients

1 ripe banana

2 ripe peaches (or 1 15-ounce can
   of peaches if not in season)

2 cups 2 percent milk

1 cup plain yogurt

½ teaspoon pure vanilla extract

1 cup crushed ice cubes

Equipment

Blender

Measuring cups

Measuring spoons

Sharp knife

Cutting board

Can opener

Cups for serving

Directions

1 Slice banana and peaches into small pieces; add to blender and blend on high speed for ten seconds. Shut off blender.

2 Add remaining ingredients and blend until smooth. Shut off blender.

Extension

In the autumn, plant peach pits in a row about 4 inches apart and 4 inches deep in soil. Cover the plantings with an inch or so of straw or mulch. Water regularly (including during the winter when conditions allow). In the spring, transplant the seedlings to large pots, or replant them where you want the trees to grow.

A Book to Read

Read the story about *James and the Giant Peach* by Roald Dahl, and enjoy James's adventures while he travels on and in a very large peach.

Yield: Makes 8 servings. Serving size ½ cup.

Nutritional information for drink: 2 grams fat, 15 grams carbohydrates, 1 gram fiber, 4 grams protein.

Did You Know?

Purple grape juice is made from Concord grapes. You're not likely to find them at your local grocery store, but they can be found at local farmers' markets in many states. They are delicious in grape pie!

PURPLE COWS

Purple is a fun color! Blend milk and Concord grape juice with banana slices to make a delicious purple drink.

Ingredients

1 banana
1 cup 2 percent milk
¼ cup Concord grape juice

Equipment

Blender
Sharp knife
Measuring cups
Cutting board
Cups for serving

Directions

1 Slice banana into bite-size pieces; add to blender.

2 Add milk and grape juice.

3 Blend on high speed for ten seconds until smooth. Shut blender off.

4 Serve in cups.

Extension

Here are some ideas for art explorations and the color purple.

- Provide a variety of purple materials, such as construction paper, ribbon, and fabric. Give the children glue or tape to assemble their masterpieces.
- Make purple drawings on butcher paper taped to cover a wall.
- Sponge paint with different shades of purple.
- At an easel, provide red and blue paint so the children can experiment with mixing the colors to create purple.

A Book to Read

Follow Harold as he journeys outside under the moonlight in the board book of Crockett Johnson's classic *Harold and the Purple Crayon*.

Yield: Makes 3 servings. Serving size ½ cup.
Nutritional information for drink: 2 grams fat, 17 grams carbohydrates, 1 gram fiber, 4 grams protein.

Did You Know?

- Cows drink 35 gallons of water each day! That is equivalent to a bathtub full of water.

- Cows produce more milk when they listen to music! Some researchers suggest that cows should listen to classical music.

SUNSHINE SHAKES

Orange juice blended with milk and a little vanilla is a great wake-up shake for children as an early morning beverage.

Ingredients

1 cup frozen orange juice concentrate, thawed
¾ cup water
¾ cup 2 percent milk
1 teaspoon pure vanilla extract

Equipment

Blender
Measuring cups
Measuring spoons
Cups for serving

Directions

1 Place all ingredients in a blender.

2 Blend on high speed until smooth. Shut off blender.

3 Serve in cups.

Extension

• Using yellow and orange paint, have the children create a circle of handprints on newspaper or butcher paper. No two sunshine rays will be the same!

• Make sunshine drawings, paintings, collages, and so on.

A Book to Read

You Are My Sunshine by Jimmie Davis illustrates a song everyone loves to sing. Perfect for a sing-along!

Yield: Makes 5 servings. Serving size ½ cup.
Nutritional information for shake: 1 gram fat, 24 grams carbohydrates, 0 grams fiber, 3 grams protein.

Did You Know?

In the past, blueberries were used for medicinal purposes.
They were used to treat coughs.

SUPER BERRY SMOOTHIE

Blend yogurt, milk, and berries to make a super smoothie. The fruit flavor possibilities are endless. Try using different flavors of yogurt too.

Ingredients

1 ripe banana

1 cup fresh or frozen mixed berries, thawed

½ cup 2 percent milk

½ cup yogurt

2 cups crushed ice cubes

Equipment

Blender

Measuring cups

Measuring spoons

Sharp knife

Cutting board

Cups for serving

Directions

1 Slice banana into bite-size pieces and place in blender.

2 Add berries, milk, and yogurt.

3 Blend on high for ten seconds. Shut off blender.

4 Add ice cubes and blend on high speed until smooth. Shut off blender.

5 Serve in cups.

Extension

There are so many different berries to taste! At a grocery store or farmers' market in season, purchase a variety of fresh berries, including raspberries, blueberries, strawberries, cranberries, and blackberries. Encourage the children to taste each kind of berry. Make a chart showing which flavors were most popular with the children.

A Book to Read

Blueberries for Sal by Robert McCloskey is an award-winning story about a little girl named Sal who is picking blueberries when she comes upon a baby bear eating blueberries. Where are their mothers?

Yield: Makes 8 servings. Serving size ½ cup.

Nutritional information for smoothie: 1 gram fat, 8 grams carbohydrates, 1 gram fiber, 2 grams protein.

Did You Know?

Summer lasts about three months. It usually begins
on June 21 and ends around September 22.

SUMMER FRUIT SMOOTHIE

A delicious way to enjoy a variety of fruits all in one fun smoothie.

Ingredients

1 banana
6 fresh strawberries
1 cup fresh raspberries
1 cup plain yogurt
1 cup pineapple juice
2 cups crushed ice cubes

Equipment

Blender
Measuring cups
Sharp knife
Cutting board
Cups for serving

Directions

1 Cut banana into bite-size pieces and place them in blender.

2 Cut green tops off each strawberry and discard them.

3 Slice each strawberry in half and place halves in blender.

4 Add raspberries, yogurt, pineapple juice, and ice cubes to the blender.

5 Mix on high speed until smooth. Shut off blender.

6 Serve in cups.

Extension

What would your smoothie be like if you didn't add ice cubes? Try it and see if you are right.

A Book to Read

Celebrate summertime by reading Bob Raczka's *Summer Wonders*, with its delightful rhyming text and attractive illustrations.

Yield: Makes 8 servings. Serving size ½ cup.
Nutritional information for smoothie: 1 gram fat, 14 grams carbohydrates, 2 grams fiber, 2 grams protein.

Did You Know?

A pineapple plant produces one pineapple per year. Pineapples weigh between three and nine pounds on average but can reach weights up to twenty pounds.

APPLE COLADA

This delicious combination of apple juice, pineapple juice, and coconut milk makes you feel like you are on a sandy beach in the Caribbean.

Ingredients

½ cup apple juice
½ cup crushed pineapple in juice
¼ cup coconut milk
½ cup crushed ice

Equipment

Measuring cups
Blender
Cups for serving

Directions

1 Place all the ingredients in a blender.

2 Blend on high speed until smooth. Shut off blender.

3 Serve in cups.

Extension

What other types of fruit coladas can you make?

A Book to Read

Join the bunny family as they visit an apple orchard and learn interesting facts about apples in Nancy Elizabeth Wallace's book *Apples, Apples, Apples*.

Yield: Makes 2 servings. Serving size ½ cup.
Nutritional information for colada: 6 grams fat, 17 grams carbohydrates, 1 gram fiber, 1 gram protein.

Did You Know?

Watermelons need bees to grow! Honeybees pollinate watermelon plants' yellow blossoms. The melon is well named, for a watermelon is 92 percent water!

WATERMELON SLUSH

Mixing watermelon with honey and ice makes a delicious, slurpy slush that tastes great!

Ingredients

3 cups seedless watermelon, cubed
1 tablespoon honey
1 cup water
4 cups crushed ice cubes

Equipment

Blender
Measuring cups
Measuring spoons
Sharp knife
Cutting board
Cups for serving
Spoons

Directions

1 Cut watermelon into 3 cups of cubed pieces.

2 Place watermelon, honey, and water in a blender.

3 Blend for ten seconds. Shut off blender.

4 Add ice and mix until slushy. Shut off blender.

5 Pour mixture into plastic cups.

6 Serve with a spoon.

Extension

Watermelon is a fruit that grows on the ground. What other fruits grow on the ground? What fruits grow in trees?

A Book to Read

Read *One Watermelon Seed* by Celia Barker Lottridge, and learn about the plants and animals that live and grow in Max and Josephine's garden.

Yield: Makes 10 servings. Serving size ½ cup.
Nutritional information for slush: 0 grams fat, 5 grams carbohydrates, 0 grams fiber, 0 grams protein.

FUN WITH FRUIT

· ·

· ·

Children enjoy both the sweet and sour tastes of fresh fruits. Fruits offer a perfect opportunity for taste testing and learning! But just exactly what is fruit? It is the sweet fleshy product of a tree or plant that contains a seed or seeds and can be eaten as food. Fruits grow in a variety of ways, such as on bushes (blueberries and raspberries), vines (grapes and melons), and trees (apples and oranges).

Provide learning for children about similarities and differences among fruits. For example, learn how fruits change as they ripen. Bananas are green when they are first picked and turn yellow when ripe; blueberries begin as white berries and ripen to blue. Some fruits, like grapes and apples, come in a variety of colors on the outside.

Cooking and preparing fruit will encourage children to learn new vocabulary—pit, core, peel, sweet, sour, and delicious! Although most markets have fruits available year-round, learn about and use fresh fruits in season. Remember that fruits are a good source of vitamins such as A, C, E, and K. What a great opportunity for children to enjoy repeating the old adage "an apple a day keeps the doctor away"!

APPLE DANISH

Enjoy this delicious danish on an early fall day. A combination of applesauce and spices on an English muffin brightens up the day.

Ingredients

1 English muffin
½ teaspoon butter, softened
2 teaspoons applesauce
1 teaspoon granulated sugar
¼ teaspoon cinnamon
A few raisins (optional)

Equipment

Small mixing bowl
Spoon for mixing
Measuring spoons
Table knife
Plates for serving

Directions

1 Carefully cut English muffin in half into two circles.

2 Spread butter on top of the muffin halves.

3 Spread applesauce over the butter.

4 In a small mixing bowl combine sugar and cinnamon.

5 Sprinkle sugar-cinnamon mixture over muffin.

6 Add raisins to the top of the muffin.

Extension

How does a cinnamon stick go from a solid to a powder?

A Book to Read

Cinnamon's Busy Year by Tony Waters is the story of a mouse named Cinnamon and her friends as they celebrate special days and holidays throughout an entire year.

Yield: Makes 2 servings. Serving size ½ English muffin.
Nutritional information for Danish: 2 grams fat, 16 grams carbohydrates, 1 gram fiber, 2 grams protein.

Did You Know?

The rice in rice cakes is cooked a lot like popcorn! Unlike popcorn, which has an outer skin or shell, rice is heated under pressure until it pops.

BANANA STACKS

Children are encouraged to enjoy food preparation and display while making this banana recipe, but remind them their mouths can only open so wide!

Ingredients

1 banana
3 mini rice cakes (plain or flavored)
1½ teaspoons fruit-flavored cream cheese
Whole pieces of fresh small fruits (blueberry, strawberry, raspberry, etc.)

Equipment

Measuring spoons
Sharp knife
Cutting board
Plates to serve on

Directions

1 Cut a banana into ½-inch slices.

2 Spread some cream cheese on a mini rice cake.

3 Add a piece of sliced banana on top of the cream cheese.

4 Top with another rice cake.

5 Continue with another layer of cream cheese, a banana slice, and then a mini rice cake.

6 Add a whole or halved piece of fruit on the top of the final layer.

Extension

Create a chart showing the different patterns and sequences of layers that are possible.

A Book to Read

A great story to tie in with bananas is *Chimps Don't Wear Glasses* by Laura Numeroff. Read about all the crazy things animals should *not* do.

Yield: Makes 1 serving. Serving size 1 "stack" of three rice cakes.
Nutritional information for banana stacks: 3 grams fat, 37 grams carbohydrates, 4 grams fiber, 3 grams protein.

BUTTERFLY SALAD

Make a nice healthy snack that looks like a butterfly by using fruit, vegetables, and cottage cheese. Serve with Fairy Tale Punch!

Ingredients

2 percent cottage cheese
Food coloring (red, yellow, and blue)
Lettuce leaf
Celery stalk
2 pineapple rings
1 large black olive
Red pepper strips

Equipment

Measuring spoons
Table knife
Cutting board
6 small bowls
Paper plates for serving

Directions

1 Mix cottage cheese and food coloring in the bowls. The colors of the cottage cheese should include both primary and secondary colors: red, yellow, blue, orange, green, and purple.

2 Place lettuce leaf on a paper plate.

3 Place celery stalk in the middle of the lettuce leaf to represent the body.

4 Slice pineapple rings in half to use as outlines of the butterfly's wings. Place curved side of pineapple halves on the sides of the celery stalk.

5 Add black olive for the head.

6 Add two red pepper strips for the antennae.

7 Place a scoop of at least 2 teaspoons of colored cottage cheese next to each pineapple's inside ring.

Extension

Give each child a sheet of construction paper. Have them color designs on both sides of the paper. After the children are finished, fold each paper accordion style. Tie one end of a three-foot length of yarn around the center of the accordion folded paper. Fan out the sides to make wings. The children can take their own butterflies outside and run in an open space to make them fly.

A Book to Read

Could you eat as much as a caterpillar? In Eric Carle's *The Very Hungry Caterpillar*, you'll see how much the caterpillar eats, and how many days it takes.

Yield: Makes 1 serving.
Nutritional information for butterfly salad: 2 grams fat, 18 grams carbohydrates, 1 gram fiber, 7 grams protein.

Did You Know?

Apples, which are grown in all fifty states, are a member of the rose family. The record for the largest apple picked is three pounds!

FILLED APPLE RINGS

Here is a new twist for the everyday apple. Extra flavor is hidden in the middle of the apple.

Ingredients

1 apple
Peanut butter, either crunchy or
     smooth, or cream cheese
     (Warning: Check for peanut
     allergies children might have!)
Raisins (optional)

Equipment

Sharp knife
Cutting board
Plates for serving
Apple corer (optional)

Directions

1 Core apple using an apple corer or a sharp knife.

2 Fill the empty core with either peanut butter or cream cheese.

3 Place the apple on its side, and cut perpendicularly across the core to make thick rings.

4 Add raisins to the peanut butter or cream cheese if you choose.

Extension

Apples come in a variety of colors. How are they similar or different?

A Book to Read

Bad Apple: A Tale of Friendship by Edward Hemingway is a story about two friends who are teased by others who think they should not be friends. Hear about how apple and worm ignore their bullies and stay friends.

Yield: Makes 2 servings. Serving size ½ apple.
Nutritional information for filled apple rings using peanut butter: 16 grams fat, 19 grams carbohydrates, 4 grams fiber, 8 grams protein.

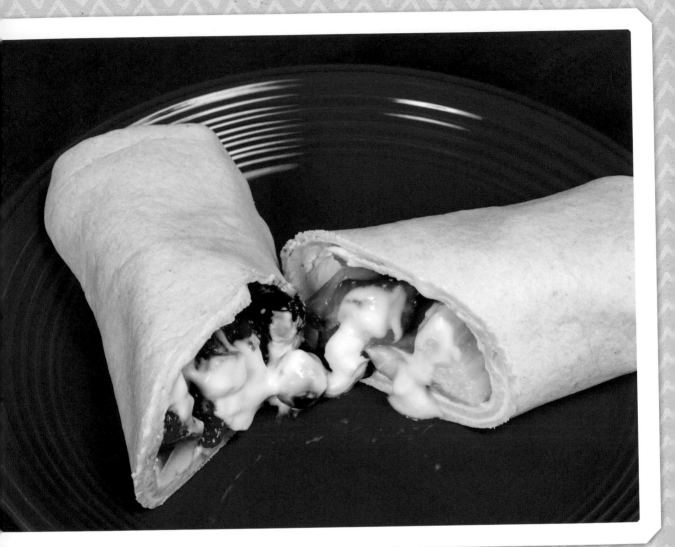

FRUIT BURRITOS

Create a rainbow in a burrito with fruits of many colors. Learning to fold the burrito is half the fun!

Ingredients

1 banana, sliced
4 strawberries, sliced
1 peach, pitted, peeled, and sliced
¼ cup fresh blueberries
1 10-inch flour tortilla
1 tablespoon cream cheese
1 tablespoon vanilla yogurt

Equipment

Measuring cups
Measuring spoons
Sharp knife
Cutting board
Table knife
Spoon
Plates for serving

Directions

1 Slice bananas, strawberries, and the peach into small thin pieces, and set aside.

2 On a tortilla, spread approximately 1 tablespoon of cream cheese.

3 Place the sliced fruit and whole blueberries down the center of the tortilla.

4 Drizzle 1 tablespoon of yogurt over the fruit.

5 Roll the tortilla burrito style. To shape the burrito, first fold the bottom edge of a softened tortilla up and over the filling. While holding the bottom of the tortilla over the filling, fold in the sides. Then, starting from the folded bottom edge, roll up the tortilla to encase the filling.

Extension

What other types of heat free burritos can you make?

A Book to Read

Learn math and Spanish at the same time while you read *Build a Burrito* by Denise Vega.

Yield: Makes 2 servings. Serving size ½ burrito.
Nutritional information for burrito: 6 grams fat, 45 grams carbohydrates, 5 grams fiber, 5 grams protein.

MERRY-GO-ROUNDS

Use animal crackers and pretzel sticks to make your own unique merry-go-round.

· ·

Ingredients

1 small apple
Peanut butter or cream cheese
   (Warning: Check for peanut allergies
   children might have!)
Animal crackers
Pretzel sticks

Equipment

Sharp knife
Table knife
Cutting board
Plates for serving

Directions

1 Cut apple crosswise in half.

2 Spread peanut butter or cream cheese over the exposed flesh (not skin) of the apple.

3 Add pretzel sticks (poles) and animal crackers by the poles.

Extension

Have you ever seen a merry-go-round? What animals did you see? Did you ride on the merry-go-round?

A Book to Read

Read *Up and Down on the Merry-Go-Round* by Bill Martin Jr. and John Archambault, a book that adds more to the merry-go-round than just horses.

· ·

Yield: Makes 2 servings. Serving size ½ apple.
Nutritional information for merry-go-rounds with peanut butter: 18 grams fat, 33 grams carbohydrates, 4 grams fiber, 10 grams protein.

Did You Know?

Most of us eat bananas upside down! The banana actually grows with the stem pointing down. By opening the banana at the other end, you'll find that you get fewer "strings" than you do if you peel from the stem. Primates like gorillas and other monkeys always peel a banana from the small end. Humans are the only ones known to peel bananas from the stem end.

MONKEY MEALS

Using peanut butter or cream cheese rather than mustard creates a perfect banana meal in a bun.

Ingredients

1 banana

1 hot dog roll

1 tablespoon peanut butter or cream cheese (Warning: Check for peanut allergies children might have!)

Slices of fruits or vegetables

Equipment

Measuring spoon

Table knife

Sharp knife

Cutting board

Bowls for fruit or vegetable slices

Plates for serving

Directions

1 Cut fruits and vegetables into long slices, and set aside.

2 Peel banana and place in hot dog roll.

3 Spread peanut butter or cream cheese over the banana.

4 Add vegetable or fruit slices as condiments.

5 Serve on a plate.

Extension

Monkeys use their tails as a fifth limb while swinging in trees. What would you do if you had a tail?

A Book to Read

Read about all the fun adventures the new teacher brings to the classroom in *The Day the Teacher Went Bananas* by James Howe.

Yield: Makes 1 serving.

Nutritional information for monkey meal with peanut butter: 10 grams fat, 50 grams carbohydrates, 6 grams fiber, 8 grams protein.

Did You Know?

In China, the peach is a symbol of longevity and good luck. In the United States, Georgia is nicknamed the Peach State because of the tasty peaches grown there.

PEACH CRISP

Here's a crispy snack you can make without an oven. Adding granola to the peaches adds a crispy texture.

Ingredients

2 8-ounce cans of diced peaches in light syrup, drained

⅛ teaspoon cinnamon

½ cup crushed granola or granola cereal (Try the granola recipe on page 77.)

½ cup vanilla yogurt

Equipment

Small mixing bowl
Measuring cups
Measuring spoons
Mixing spoon
Can opener
Small bowls for serving
Spoons for eating

Directions

1 Place peaches in a small bowl, and stir in cinnamon.

2 Divide fruit and cinnamon mixture between four serving bowls, ½ cup per bowl.

3 Sprinkle each serving with 2 tablespoons of granola.

4 Top each serving with 2 tablespoons of yogurt.

5 Sprinkle more cinnamon on top if desired.

Extension

Nectarines are much like peaches without the fuzzy peel. Have children compare a peach with a nectarine, and list their observations about what is different and what is the same. How do their tastes compare?

A Book to Read

The ABCs of Fruits and Vegetables and Beyond by Steve Charney and David Goldbeck is full of facts, jokes, silly sayings, and recipes.

Yield: Makes 4 servings. Serving size ½ cup fruit.

Nutritional information for peach crisp: 4 grams fat, 31 grams carbohydrates, 3 grams fiber, 4 grams protein.

SHAKE AND NO-BAKE APPLES

Shake up some sliced apple rounds with cinnamon and brown sugar for a yummy apple treat.

Ingredients

1 apple
½ teaspoon cinnamon
⅛ cup brown sugar

Equipment

Measuring cups
Measuring spoon
Knives
Apple corer (optional)
Cutting board
Gallon-size ziplock bag
Plates for serving

Directions

1 Core the apple.

2 Cut the apple into 6 pieces.

3 Place brown sugar and cinnamon in a ziplock plastic bag.

4 Add apples and shake until they are all coated.

5 Serve on small plates.

Extension

What is the difference between white sugar and brown sugar? Learn by making your own brown sugar. In a medium-size bowl, mix together 1 cup of granulated cane sugar with 1 tablespoon of unsulfured molasses. The molasses will start out clumpy, but don't worry. Keep mixing it together, and it will all even out. Store in an airtight container. Now you know all about brown sugar!

A Book to Read

Jill Braithwaite's book *From Cane to Sugar* explores the process of how sugar is made from sugarcane.

Yield: Makes 2 servings. Serving size 3 apple slices.
Nutritional information for apples: 0 grams fat, 49 grams carbohydrates, 3 grams fiber, 0 grams protein.

Did You Know?

About 25 percent of an apple's volume is air.
That's why apples float!

WHIPPED CREAM FRUIT SALAD

A variety of fruit pieces are combined with whipping cream and orange juice to make a fruit salad. Children will see how a liquid becomes a solid, how orange juice keeps fruits from bruising, and how to fold the ingredients together.

Ingredients

1 cup heavy whipping cream
2 medium apples
2 medium bananas
½ cup orange juice
1½ cups seedless grapes

Equipment

Mixing bowl, chilled
Electric hand mixer or whisk
Mixing spoon
Measuring cups
Sharp knife
Cutting board
Bowls for serving
Spoons for eating

Directions

1 Chill mixing bowl, beaters or whisk, and whipping cream before you begin.

2 Dice apples and dip them into orange juice to keep them from turning brown; set aside.

3 Cut bananas into bite-size pieces and dip them into orange juice to keep them from turning brown; set aside.

4 In the chilled mixing bowl whip the cream until it forms stiff peaks.

5 Gently fold all the fruit into the thick cream and then serve in small bowls.

Extension

What other fruits float like apples? Chart your results on a graph.

A Book to Read

Read how Oliver picks the fruit from his grandfather's garden and learns to love eating fruit salad in *Oliver's Fruit Salad* by Vivian French.

Yield: Makes 10 servings. Serving size ½ cup.
Nutritional information for fruit salad: 9 grams fat, 15 grams carbohydrates, 1 gram fiber, 1 gram protein.

Did You Know?
Strawberries are part of the rose family.

STRAWBERRY SHORTCAKE SANDWICHES

Here's a twist on a traditional strawberry treat. Enjoy strawberry shortcake during May, National Strawberry Month.

Ingredients

Frozen pound cake (10 ounces), thawed

2 cups of strawberries

¼ cup granulated sugar

½ cup whipped cream (see page 13 for recipe)

Equipment

Measuring cups

Measuring spoons

Mixing bowl

Mixing spoon

Sharp knife

Cutting board

Plates for serving

Directions

1 Cut pound cake into ½-inch slices (approximately 14 slices).

2 Wash strawberries, and remove and discard stems (also called hulls).

3 Slice strawberries, and put them in a mixing bowl.

4 Stir in ¼ cup sugar, and mix well. Cover with plastic wrap, and set aside. (Stir frequently to make the juice.)

5 Place 1 cake piece on a plate. Place 4 tablespoons strawberries and juice on top of the cake piece.

6 Top with another piece of pound cake.

7 Pour another 4 tablespoons of strawberries and juice on top of the cake layer.

8 Top with 2 teaspoons of whipped topping.

Extension

How much juice do the strawberries make? Set a timer, and record how much juice is made every ten minutes. Remember to stir the strawberries frequently.

A Book to Read

The Little Mouse, The Red Ripe Strawberry, and The Big Hungry Bear by Don and Audrey Wood is a story about a little mouse who tries to hide his strawberry from a bear!

Yield: Makes 7 servings. Serving size 1 sandwich.

Nutritional information for shortcake: 11 grams fat, 30 grams carbohydrates, 1 gram fiber, 3 grams protein.

Did You Know?

Lemon juice can be used to keep some fruits, such as apples and bananas, from becoming brown.

WALDORF SALAD POCKETS

This pita pocket salad combines apples, grapes, and cranberries mixed with vanilla yogurt for a quick salad on the go.

Ingredients

½ green apple (Granny Smith or similar), cored and diced

½ red apple (Red Delicious or similar), cored and diced

3 tablespoons dried cranberries

¼ cup seedless red grapes, chopped

½ celery stick, sliced

½ teaspoon lemon juice

½ cup vanilla yogurt

3 pitas

1 teaspoon chopped walnuts (optional) (Warning: Check for nut allergies children might have!)

Equipment

Mixing bowl

Mixing spoon

Measuring cups

Measuring spoons

Cutting board

Sharp knife

Apple corer (optional)

Directions

1 Place diced apple pieces in a mixing bowl.

2 Add cranberries, grapes, and celery.

3 Pour lemon juice over the mixture, and stir well.

4 Pour yogurt over fruit, and stir well to combine.

5 If you are using walnuts, add them now, and mix well.

6 Cut pitas in half across the diameter, and open the pocket.

7 Fill each pita half with the fruit mixture.

8 Serve on a plate or napkin.

Extension
What happens inside a pita that creates a pocket while it is cooking?

A Book to Read
Read about all the different types of bread that we eat in *Bread, Bread, Bread* by Ann Morris.

Yield: Makes 6 servings. Serving size ½ filled pita.

Nutritional information for pockets: 2 grams fat, 29 grams carbohydrates, 2 grams fiber, 4 grams protein.

Chapter 4

SNACKS

· ·

· ·

The snacks in this chapter are nutritious and healthy compared to the junk-food snacks many children eat. The recipes include fresh and dried fruits, fresh vegetables, granola, and yogurt.

The granolas and mixes will allow children to experience tastes and textures such as sweet, sour, chewy, and crunchy. They will be exposed to subtraction and fractions through altering the recipes to change the serving quantities. New vocabulary will include the words *mashing* and *packed*.

The recipes in the puddings and mousses section develop children's problem-solving skills as they choose what ingredients they would like for parfaits and figure out how to create new colors for rainbow pudding. These recipes provide much healthier puddings than those made from mixes or purchased ready to serve.

Children will have the opportunity to make sandwiches and salads that are usually made ahead of time. When they make the "walking salad," they will be excited to discover that you don't always have to eat a salad out of a bowl!

Did You Know?

In 1876 Dr. John Harvey Kellogg (of Kellogg Cereal fame) was experimenting with various foods and developed "granula." He eventually changed the name to *granola*.

GRANOLA

Granola is nutritious, but this one is scrumptious too! For a sweeter granola, add more honey. For a crunchier granola, add more nuts. For a chewier granola, add more fruit.

Ingredients

2 cups uncooked oatmeal

½ cup shredded coconut

½ cup wheat germ

½ cup chopped unsalted peanuts
(Warning: Check for peanut or other nut allergies children might have!)

½ cup chopped dried fruit

½ cup sunflower seeds

¼ teaspoon nutmeg

½ cup honey

Equipment

Mixing bowl

Mixing spoon

Measuring cups

Measuring spoons

Sharp knife

Cutting board

Food storage container with lid

Cups or bowls for serving

Directions

1 Mix all of the dry ingredients together in a large mixing bowl until they are blended evenly.

2 Add honey, and stir until the dry ingredients are evenly coated.

3 Store in an airtight container.

Extension

What other ingredients could you add to the granola? How would it change the flavor?

A Book to Read

Nutmeg and Barley: A Budding Friendship by Janie Bynum tells the story of a squirrel named Nutmeg and a mouse named Barley. A surprise leads to an unlikely friendship between the two.

Yield: Makes 20 servings. Serving size ¼ cup.

Nutritional information for granola: 5 grams fat, 16 grams carbohydrates, 2 grams fiber, 3 grams protein.

Did You Know?

To make one 12-ounce jar of peanut butter, you need about 540 peanuts. According to the National Peanut Board, 60 percent of consumers prefer creamy peanut butter over chunky.

CRUNCHOLA

This is a crunchy treat for snacktime. Mixing granola with chocolate chips and raisins makes a tasty combination.

Ingredients

½ cup crunchy or smooth peanut butter (Warning: Check for peanut or other nut allergies children might have!)

½ cup butter, softened

1 cup oats

1 cup puffed rice cereal

½ cup chocolate chips

½ cup raisins

¼ teaspoon pure vanilla extract

Equipment

Mixing bowl

Mixing spoon

Measuring cups

Measuring spoons

Cookie sheet

Fork

Wax paper

Plates for serving

Directions

1 Using a fork, mash together butter and peanut butter in a mixing bowl.

2 Stir in oats, puffed rice cereal, chocolate chips, raisins, and vanilla extract. Mix well.

3 Roll into bite-size balls; place balls on wax paper on a cookie sheet.

4 Chill for an hour, and then serve.

5 Consider using granola instead of oatmeal (see the granola recipe on page 77).

Extension

Take a classroom poll to find out how many children prefer creamy peanut butter and how many prefer chunky peanut butter. Make a table or graph showing the results.

A Book to Read

Curious George Goes to a Chocolate Factory by Margret Rey and H. A. Rey is a chocolate adventure for Curious George and the man in the yellow hat!

Yield: Makes 14 servings. Serving size ¼ cup.

Nutritional information for crunchola: 14 grams fat, 17 grams carbohydrates, 2 grams fiber, 4 grams protein.

Did You Know?

Food drying is also called *food dehydration*, which is the process of removing water from food.

MONKEY MIX

Tropical dried fruits mix together to make a tasty treat that is so yummy it won't last long. Good thing that it's so quick and easy to make!

Ingredients

1¼ cups dried bananas

1 cup dried papaya

1 cup dried mango

¼ cup sliced almonds (Warning: Check for nut allergies children might have!)

¼ cup shredded coconut

¼ cup mini chocolate chips

Equipment

Mixing bowl

Mixing spoon

Measuring cups

Ziplock plastic bags or food storage container with lid

Bowls for serving

Directions

1 Combine all ingredients in a large mixing bowl and mix well.

2 Store in ziplock plastic bags or a food storage container with lid to keep fresh.

Extension

Try taste testing these recipes with fresh fruit rather than dried fruit. What differences are there?

A Book to Read

Kama and Nani live in Hawaii. They love to help their grandpa pick mangos from the mango tree! But there are too many in *Too Many Mangos* by Tammy Paikai. What will Kama and Nani do with all the mangos?

Yield: Makes 16 servings. Serving size ¼ cup.

Nutritional information for monkey mix: 3 grams fat, 23 grams carbohydrates, 3 grams fiber, 2 grams protein.

Did You Know?

Raisins are dry grapes. After grapes have been picked, they are laid out to dry in the sun for two to three weeks. They become raisins.

SQUIRREL MIX

This mix combines sunflower seeds, almonds, dried fruits, and cereal for a scrumptious anytime snack.

Ingredients

1 cup hulled sunflower seeds
½ cup sliced almonds (Warning: Check for nut allergies children might have!)
½ cup dried cranberries
½ cup golden raisins, packed
½ cup oat Os cereal

Equipment

Mixing bowl
Measuring cups
Ziplock plastic bag or food storage container with lid
Cups or bowls for serving

Directions

1 Place all ingredients in a large mixing bowl and mix well.

2 Store in a ziplock plastic bag or in a food storage container with a lid.

Extension

What types of nuts fall from trees for squirrels to eat?

A Book to Read

In *The Busy Little Squirrel* by Nancy Tafuri, Squirrel is getting ready for winter. As he travels looking for food, he meets up with his friends, who have other ideas about things to do.

Yield: Makes 12 servings. Serving size ¼ cup.
Nutritional information for squirrel mix: 9 grams fat, 14 grams carbohydrates, 3 grams fiber, 4 grams protein.

PLENTY OF PARFAITS

Parfaits are fun to make and even better to eat. Making parfaits in clear cups allows you to see all the layers. Parfaits become art you can eat!

Ingredients

1 tablespoon chocolate chips

¼ cup coarse graham cracker crumbs

¼ cup yogurt

2 tablespoons raisins

2 tablespoons whipped cream (see recipe on page 13)

Equipment

Measuring cups

Measuring spoons

Small bowls for different ingredients

9-ounce clear plastic cups for serving

Spoons for eating

Directions

1 Place chocolate chips in cup.

2 Cover chocolate chips with graham cracker crumbs.

3 Spoon yogurt over graham cracker crumbs.

4 Top yogurt with raisins.

5 Add a dollop of whipped cream on top of raisins.

Variations

You can create thousands of different parfaits. Here's a list of possible ingredients to get you started.

- whipped cream
- frozen orange juice
- nuts (Warning: Check for nut allergies children might have!)
- graham crackers
- chocolate chips
- applesauce
- yogurt
- granola (see recipe on page 77)
- cereal
- pineapple chunks
- custard
- raisins
- jelly
- fruit cocktail
- jam or preserves

Extension

How many layers does your parfait have? Chart children's responses and make comparisons.

A Book to Read

Join young grape and grandpa raisin as they enjoy each other's company in *Raisin and Grape* by Tom Amico and James Proimos.

Yield: Makes 1 serving. Serving size 1 cup.

Nutritional information for parfait: 12 grams fat, 45 grams carbohydrates, 2 grams fiber, 6 grams protein.

Did You Know?

What are the colors in a rainbow? Roy G. Biv is a made-up name that uses the first letter of each rainbow color to help people remember. **R**ed, **O**range, **Y**ellow, **G**reen, **B**lue, **I**ndigo, and **V**iolet. R O Y G B I V!

RAINBOW PUDDING

Everyone loves a rainbow, and this pudding is a rainbow you can eat! Hide a teddy graham cookie at the bottom of the cup, and pretend it is gold! Colored vanilla yogurt is the secret ingredient.

Ingredients

3 8-ounce containers of vanilla yogurt
Food coloring (red, yellow, and blue)

Equipment

6 small bowls
Teaspoons for stirring and eating
Clear plastic cups

Directions

1 Divide yogurt into 6 bowls.

2 In one bowl add 9 drops of red food coloring, and mix well.

3 In another bowl add 9 drops of yellow food coloring, and mix well.

4 In a third bowl add 9 drops of blue food coloring, and mix well.

5 In a fourth bowl add 6 drops of red food coloring and 3 drops of yellow food coloring. Mix well to make orange.

6 In a fifth bowl add 6 drops of yellow food coloring and 3 drops of blue food coloring. Mix well to make green.

7 In the last bowl add 6 drops of red food coloring and 3 drops of blue food coloring. Mix well to make purple.

8 In a plastic cup place 2 tablespoons of each colored pudding in layers, and then eat.

Extension

Offer paint in primary colors, and encourage children to mix paints to create the secondary colors. Primary colors are red, yellow, and blue. Secondary colors are orange, green, and purple.

A Book to Read

Find more rainbow colors in the book *The Mixed-Up Chameleon* by Eric Carle, which follows the chameleon's adventures at the zoo.

Yield: Makes 4 servings. Serving size ¾ cup.
Nutritional information for rainbow pudding: 2 grams fat, 25 grams carbohydrates, 0 grams fiber, 9 grams protein.

BANANA PUDDING

Children can make this nutritious pudding all by themselves. Be ready to serve seconds!

Ingredients

2 ripe bananas

¼ cup applesauce

2 tablespoons honey

Equipment

Measuring cup

Measuring spoons

Small mixing bowl

Fork

Rubber spatula

Bowls for serving

Spoons

Directions

1 Mash bananas with a fork until soft.

2 Add applesauce and honey. Mix until smooth.

3 Chill for an hour, and then serve.

Extension

Do a taste testing of different bananas, such as baby bananas, plantain bananas, and red bananas. Have children share their thoughts about the different bananas.

A Book to Read

In *Jungle School* by Elizabeth Laird, a little monkey named Jani is starting at a new school, and she is nervous about how her monkey classmates will react to her wheelchair.

Yield: Makes 4 servings. Serving size ¼ cup.

Nutritional information for banana pudding: 0 grams fat, 25 grams carbohydrates, 2 grams fiber, 1 gram protein.

Did You Know?

About 96 percent of people put the peanut butter on the bread before the jelly when making a peanut butter and jelly sandwich.

SANDWICH ROLL-UPS

Roll-ups offer a new way to eat a sandwich! Flatten a slice of bread with a rolling pin, and then roll it up around your choice of fillings.

Ingredients

1 slice of bread

1 teaspoon peanut butter (Warning: Check for peanut or other nut allergies children might have!)

2 teaspoons jelly, jam, or preserves

Equipment

Rolling pin

Wax paper

Measuring spoons

Plates for serving

Toothpicks (optional)

Directions

1 Using a rolling pin, roll out a slice of bread on wax paper until it is very thin.

2 Spread peanut butter over the bread.

3 Spread jelly on top of the peanut butter.

4 Carefully roll bread lengthwise. Use toothpicks to hold it together if needed.

5 Slice into bite-size pieces or eat whole.

Variations

Create your own filling for a roll-up. Here are some ideas.

- peanut butter (Warning: Check for peanut or other nut allergies children might have!)
- jelly
- ham
- cheese
- chicken salad
- bologna
- tuna
- beef
- tomato
- lettuce
- pickles
- shredded carrots

Extension

How long is your sandwich roll-up? Use a ruler to measure it.

A Book to Read

Make an imaginary peanut butter and jelly sandwich while reading *Peanut Butter and Jelly: A Play Rhyme* by Nadine Bernard Westcott.

Yield: Makes 1 serving.

Nutritional information for sandwich: 9 grams fat, 33 grams carbohydrates, 2 grams fiber, 6 grams protein.

Did You Know?

Did Little Miss Muffet eat her cottage cheese? Yes!
She was eating her "curds and whey," which are the
lumps and liquid found in cottage cheese.

WALKING SALAD FOR ONE

Enjoy an apple salad as a simple snack or a full meal, even when you are on the go.

Ingredients

1 apple

2 teaspoons cottage cheese

6 raisins

6 peanuts, chopped (Warning: Check
   for peanut or other nut allergies
   children might have!)

1 teaspoon mayonnaise

Equipment

Small mixing bowl

Measuring spoons

Cutting board

Spoon

Sharp knife

Apple corer (optional)

Directions

1 Cut off the top of the apple.

2 Core it almost all the way through using an apple corer or a sharp knife.

3 Scoop out the remaining pulp, and chop it up well.

4 In a small mixing bowl, mix apple pulp with cottage cheese, raisins, nuts, and mayonnaise.

5 Put the apple mixture into the apple shell, and put the top back on it.

6 Eat as a snack, a meal on the go, or as a light, nutritious meal—even breakfast.

Extension

Go on a scavenger hunt while enjoying your walking salad. You can have a hunt indoors or outdoors!

A Book to Read

Walking through the Jungle by Debbie Harter explores the wonders of the rain forest through the eyes of a young girl.

Yield: Makes 1 serving.

Nutritional information for walking salad: 8 grams fat, 29 grams carbohydrates, 5 grams fiber, 3 grams protein.

Did You Know?

Some people believe that lettuce makes you sleepy, so they serve it at the end of the meal to help those who eat it fall asleep easily at bedtime.

GREEK SALAD

Feta cheese turns this refreshing salad into a great alternative to commonplace salad. It is made with chopped tomatoes, cucumbers, and green peppers. Imported feta cheese is usually made with goat's or sheep's milk, as is the original Greek feta cheese.

Ingredients

For the salad:

6 cups torn lettuce (iceberg or romaine)
2 small tomatoes, cored and cut into wedges
1 medium cucumber, peeled and sliced
1 green pepper, cored, seeded, and cut into rings
4 ounces feta cheese
⅔ cup oregano dressing

For the dressing:

2 cups olive oil
3 tablespoons red wine vinegar
1 tablespoon dried oregano
½ teaspoon salt
¼ teaspoon black pepper

Equipment

Measuring cups
Measuring spoons
Large mixing bowl
Small mixing bowl
Sharp knife
Cutting board
Whisk
Small bowls for serving
Forks
Corer (optional)

Directions

1 Tear lettuce into large mixing bowl.

2 Cut tomatoes and cucumber, place them in large mixing bowl, and toss.

3 Add green peppers and feta cheese, and toss again. (Warning: Have children wash their hands after handling peppers; and make sure they avoid touching their faces until they do so.)

4 To make the dressing, add all dressing ingredients to small mixing bowl.

5 Using a whisk, mix dressing ingredients until well blended.

6 Top the salad with ⅔ cup dressing, toss again, then serve.

7 Store extra dressing in the refrigerator in a food storage container.

Extension

Greece has about two thousand islands. Its largest island is Crete.

A Book to Read

Learn more about the alphabet, vegetables, and fruits in *An Alphabet Salad: Fruits and Vegetables from A to Z* by Sarah L. Schuette.

Yield: Makes 36 servings. Serving size ¼ cup.
Nutritional information for Greek salad with dressing: 5 grams fat, 1 gram carbohydrates, 0 grams fiber, 1 gram protein.

CINNAMON ROLLS

This recipe is a version of sandwich roll–ups with a little twist. Adding butter and a brown sugar mix results in an old favorite.

Ingredients

2 slices of bread
2 teaspoons butter
1 tablespoon brown or white sugar
½ teaspoon cinnamon

Equipment

Mixing bowl
Measuring spoons
Rolling pin
Table knife
Teaspoon
Plate

Directions

1 Roll the bread until thin.

2 Spread butter on one side of each slice.

3 Combine sugar and cinnamon and sprinkle on top of butter.

4 Carefully roll bread lengthwise. Hold together with toothpicks if needed.

5 Slice into ½-inch pieces.

Extension

You can "paint" on bread using egg yolks and food coloring.

A Book to Read

After some nibbling at his cage, Cinnamon escapes into the wide world. Enjoy his adventures as you read *Cinnamon's Day Out: A Gerbil Adventure* by Susan L. Roth.

Yield: Makes 2 servings. Serving size 1 roll-up.
Nutritional information for cinnamon rolls: 5 grams fat, 22 grams carbohydrates, 1 gram fiber, 2 grams protein.

Did You Know?

Cranberries are one of the few fruits that are native to North America. Concord grapes and blueberries are two others. Cranberries got their name from Dutch and German settlers who called them "crane berries" because the cranberry blossom looks like the head and beak of a crane.

MERRY BERRY SALAD

Here's a colorful recipe for the holidays or anytime! Mixing cranberries, apple juice, and vinegar creates a delicious dressing for this salad.

Ingredients

For the salad:

1 10-ounce bag of mixed salad greens
1 medium red apple
1 medium green apple
1 cup shredded Parmesan cheese
½ cup dried cranberries

For the dressing:

1 cup dried cranberries
½ cup sugar
½ cup cider vinegar
¼ cup apple juice concentrate
1 teaspoon salt
1 cup vegetable oil

Equipment

Mixing bowl
Mixing spoon
Measuring cups
Measuring spoons
Sharp knife
Cutting board
Blender

Directions

1 Wash salad greens, and place them in a mixing bowl.

2 Dice both apples, and add to the salad greens.

3 Add Parmesan cheese and dried cranberries, and mix well.

4 Add dressing ingredients except for the oil to a blender, and mix until it is smooth.

5 Slowly add vegetable oil to blender, and mix well.

6 Pour dressing over salad.

7 Toss salad before serving.

Extension

Cranberries come in many different forms. Compare the tastes of dried cranberries, fresh cranberries, cranberry sauce, and cranberry juice.

A Book to Read

Poor Clarence can't bounce. He tries, but he just can't do it. In *Clarence: The Cranberry Who Couldn't Bounce* by Jim Coogan, you will read how he overcomes his battle and learns to bounce.

Yield (salad): Makes 18 servings. Serving size ¼ cup.
Nutritional information for salad: 2 grams fat, 7 grams carbohydrates, 1 gram fiber, 3 grams protein.

Yield (dressing): Makes 18 servings. Serving size 2 tablespoons.
Nutritional information for dressing: 12 grams fat, 12 grams carbohydrates, 0 grams fiber, 0 grams protein.

Chapter 5

COOKIES AND PIES

· ·

· ·

Of all the things we've made together, I've always enjoyed making cookies with children the most. It gives the children an opportunity to create the recipe and to really be hands-on!

Of course the children are measuring, reading, and following directions, but when it comes to mixing, their hands are the number one piece of equipment. Allow the children to get their hands in the cookie dough so they can feel the different textures. Many of the cookie recipes have an outside coating added as the last step in the process. Again, let the children get their hands in there and shake the coating onto the cookies.

As in any good pie, the inside filling for Banana Mash is scrumptious! This recipe offers another opportunity for children to create using their hands. Mashing and mixing the ingredients together quickly add a new aroma to the air. The Fruit Pie recipe provides the children with an opportunity to see how you can use the outside of a fruit to add a tasty zest to the cream cheese.

Did You Know?

- Honey bees' wings beat about 11,400 times every minute, producing their unique buzzing sound.

- Honey bees do not sleep for long periods of time. Instead they take mini-naps throughout the day.

- And only the female worker bees make honey.

HONEY BALLS

Cornflakes, honey, peanut butter, and dry milk combine to make this scrumptious cookie.

Ingredients

1 cup cornflakes

5 tablespoons honey

5 tablespoons peanut butter (Warning: Check for peanut or other nut allergies children might have!)

½ cup dry milk

Equipment

Mixing bowl

Mixing spoon

Measuring cups

Measuring spoons

Rolling pin

Gallon-size ziplock plastic bag

Cookie sheet

Wax paper

Small plates for serving

Directions

1 Place wax paper on the cookie sheet.

2 Place cornflakes in the ziplock plastic bag, close it, and use a rolling pin to crush the flakes.

3 Mix honey, peanut butter, and dry milk well, and form the mixture into 1-inch balls.

4 Place one ball at a time into the ziplock plastic bag containing the crushed cornflake mixture, and shake the bag to coat the cookie.

5 Place the cookies on wax paper.

6 Chill for thirty minutes.

7 Store in a ziplock plastic bag.

Extension

The honeycomb cell is the shape of a hexagon. Cut out colorful hexagons to glue into unique honeycomb designs.

A Book to Read

Enjoy the rhyming text in *Love Is a Handful of Honey* by Giles Andreae, and discover how a toddler bear spends his day.

Yield: Makes 1 dozen cookies. Serving size 2 cookies.

Nutritional information for honey balls: 7 grams fat, 26 grams carbohydrates, 1 gram fiber, 7 grams protein.

Did You Know?

Monday's name comes from the Latin *dies lunae*, meaning "moon's day."

MOON BALLS

This is the first recipe I ever used in my classroom. And moon balls are still easy and very tasty!

Ingredients

1 cup raisins, packed

1 cup dry milk

2 ½ cups graham cracker crumbs
(keep ½ cup separate)

⅔ cup honey

1 cup peanut butter (Warning:
Check for peanut or other nut
allergies children might have!)

Equipment

Mixing bowl

Mixing spoon

Measuring cups

Cookie sheet

Wax paper

Gallon-size ziplock plastic bag

Small plates for serving

Directions

1 Place wax paper on cookie sheet.

2 Mix raisins, dry milk, and 2 cups graham cracker crumbs in a large mixing bowl.

3 Add honey and peanut butter. Mix well. Mixing with your hands works best.

4 Roll dough into 1-inch balls, and place them on wax paper.

5 Place ½ cup graham cracker crumbs in ziplock plastic bag.

6 Place one ball at a time in the ziplock plastic bag, and shake to coat the cookie with crumbs. Place it back on the cookie sheet.

7 Chill for thirty minutes.

8 Place leftovers in a ziplock plastic bag.

Extension

Make a "Moon Book" to illustrate the moon's different phases. Each child can take the book home for an evening to illustrate what the moon looks like. Supply white paper and crayons.

A Book to Read

Papa Please Get the Moon for Me by Eric Carle tells how much Monica wants the moon.

Yield: Makes 36 cookies. Serving size 2 cookies.

Nutritional information for moon balls: 8 grams fat, 33 grams carbohydrates, 2 grams fiber, 7 grams protein.

Did You Know?

Rice becomes crisp when it is cooked, dried, and toasted. When its temperature changes, it makes a popping sound!

CRISPY PEANUT BUTTER BALLS

I made this recipe with my mother when I was young. My brother and I couldn't wait to eat the crispy balls made with a mixture of peanut butter, honey, vanilla, and puffed rice cereal.

Ingredients

½ cup peanut butter (Warning: Check for peanut or other nut allergies children might have!)

¼ cup honey

½ teaspoon pure vanilla extract

3 cups puffed rice cereal

Equipment

Measuring cups

Measuring spoon

Mixing bowl

Mixing spoon

Rubber spatula

Cookie sheet

Wax paper

Small plates for serving

Gallon-size ziplock plastic bag

Directions

1 Place wax paper on a cookie sheet.

2 In a mixing bowl combine peanut butter, honey, and vanilla extract.

3 Using a rubber spatula, stir in cereal, and mix well.

4 Roll mixture into 1-inch balls, and place them on cookie sheet.

5 Chill for thirty minutes, and then serve.

6 Store in a ziplock plastic bag.

Extension

Offer children honey off the honeycomb, which is usually sold as a square piece or is available as chunks in jars. Visit your local farmers' markets to see if they stock honeycomb.

A Book to Read

Little Bear does not like to do much, mostly because he is afraid. But when someone needs help, he is right there despite his fears. Read more about Little Bear in *The Bear Who Didn't Like Honey* by Barbara Maitland.

Yield: Makes 12 cookies. Serving size 1 cookie.

Nutritional information for crispy peanut butter balls: 5 grams fat, 20 grams carbohydrates, 1 gram fiber, 3 grams protein.

Did You Know?

Gorillas build new sleeping nests every night. Their nests are made from branches and leaves. They can be found in trees and on the ground. Scientists use the nests to count the population of gorillas.

BANANA COOKIES

These cookies are made with fresh bananas and a touch of graham cracker crumbs. The result is a yummy and crunchy snack that is perfect for any day.

Ingredients

9 graham crackers
3 bananas

Equipment

Sharp knife
Cutting board
Rolling pin
Cookie sheet
Wax paper
Gallon-size ziplock plastic bag

Directions

1 Place wax paper on a cookie sheet.

2 Place graham crackers in the ziplock plastic bag.

3 Using a rolling pin, roll over graham crackers until they become crumbs.

4 Cut each banana into 8 pieces. First cut a banana in half, then cut each half in half, and then cut each piece in half again, leaving 8 pieces.

5 Place a few banana slices into the graham cracker crumbs and shake.

6 Place graham cracker–covered bananas on a cookie sheet.

7 Eat immediately.

8 Store cookies in a ziplock plastic bag.

Extension

Develop a gorilla unit for your classroom. There are two species of gorillas, the western gorilla and the eastern gorilla. Each species has subspecies.

Both of the western gorilla subspecies, cross river gorillas and western lowland gorillas, are on the critically endangered list.

Study the differences between the gorillas, including hair color, hair length, height, weight, population size, locations where they live, and foods that they eat.

Learn more about why gorillas are on the endangered species list by visiting the International Union for Conservation of Nature's Red List of Threatened Species website at www.iucnredlist.org.

A Book to Read

Little Gorilla is loved by everyone in the jungle, but what will happen as he grows bigger? Learn more in the book *Little Gorilla* by Ruth Bornstein.

Yield: Makes 24 cookies. Serving size 4 cookies.
Nutritional information for banana cookies: 2 grams fat, 30 grams carbohydrates, 2 grams fiber, 2 grams protein.

BANANA MASH

Mashing bananas with cream cheese and butter and adding puffed rice cereal, a little cocoa, honey, and coconut results in a smashing good pie!

Ingredients

3 very ripe bananas

3 ounces cream cheese, softened

1 tablespoon honey

4 tablespoons butter, softened

2 tablespoons cocoa powder

½ cup shredded coconut flakes

2 cups puffed rice cereal

1 graham cracker pie crust (any flavor will do)

Equipment

Mixing bowl

Mixing spoon

Measuring cups

Measuring spoon

Forks

Rubber spatula

Sharp knife

Small plates for serving

Directions

1 Mash two bananas with a fork in a mixing bowl.

2 Add cream cheese, honey, and butter to smashed bananas. Continue mashing with a fork.

3 Stir in cocoa powder and coconut, and mix until well blended.

4 Mix in puffed rice cereal.

5 Pour mixture into pie crust. Use a rubber spatula to spread it evenly.

6 Slice remaining banana into ½-inch disks, and place them on top of pie.

7 Chill or freeze for thirty minutes.

Extension

Dissect a coconut! To open one you will need a large nail, a hammer, a bath towel, and a bowl.

1. First release the coconut milk by hammering a nail into each of the three "eyes" on the coconut.

2. Let the coconut milk drip into a bowl, and set it aside for future use.

3. Next wrap the coconut up in a bath towel. Make sure it is completely covered so that the pieces don't break free.

4. Hit the coconut with a hammer a few times until it has cracked open.

5. Talk about the inside of the coconut, and taste that pulp inside. Is it different from the coconut in the recipe?

A Book to Read

In *Five Little Monkeys Go Shopping*, Eileen Christelow tells about a family of monkeys and their adventure going school shopping!

Yield: Makes 16 servings. Serving size 1 slice (⅟₁₆ of pie).

Nutritional information for banana mash: 8 grams fat, 18 grams carbohydrates, 1 gram fiber, 2 grams protein.

Did You Know?

A survey by the American Pie Council and Crisco found that apple pie is the favorite flavor for one out of four Americans. The average American eats six slices of pie a year.

FRUIT PIE

This pie has peaches and blueberries on top of cream cheese that carries a hint of orange.

Ingredients

1 29-ounce can sliced peaches
   in light syrup
8 ounces cream cheese, softened
¼ cup sugar
2 teaspoons fresh orange zest
2 tablespoons orange juice
1 graham cracker pie crust
1 cup fresh blueberries

Equipment

Mixing bowl
Mixing spoon
Measuring cups
Measuring spoons
Rubber spatula
Grater
Sharp knife
Forks
Small plates for serving

Directions

1 Drain canned sliced peaches and set aside.

2 Mix cream cheese with sugar until smooth.

3 Mix orange zest and orange juice into cream cheese until well blended.

4 Spread the cream cheese mixture into the pie crust.

5 Top with peaches and blueberries.

6 Chill one hour or overnight.

Extension

Make your own orange peel using a grater. Grate only the orange colored part. The white part is bitter and will make your pie bitter too. Measure the orange peel needed for your recipe and enjoy!

A Book to Read

Read about a special tree that grows pies. Each season you will notice something new on the tree in *Pie in the Sky* by Lois Ehlert.

Yield: Makes 16 servings. Serving size 1 slice (⅟₁₆ of pie).
Nutritional information for fruit pie: 8 grams fat, 20 grams carbohydrates, 1 gram fiber, 2 grams protein.

FROZEN TREATS

Water is the main ingredient of most foods. As a result, the process of freezing food is the process of freezing water. The recipes in this chapter incorporate the importance of following directions so that the outcome is a frozen food.

During the process of freezing, children will be able to observe and record how a liquid becomes a solid when making Ice Cream in a Bag. While making the same recipe, children will learn why adding salt to ice makes it melt.

Children will experience new tastes, such as the evaporated milk in Raspberry Orange Pops. When making the Frozen Orange Banana Yogurt Pops, children can taste bananas both before and after they are frozen.

Use pure flavorings and fresh fruits for the recipes in this chapter. You'll notice an enhanced flavor in your treats!

Did You Know?
It takes 1.375 gallons (12 pounds) of milk to make just 1 gallon of ice cream.

ICE CREAM IN A BAG

You can watch the ice cream–making process through the bag as the liquid becomes a solid. It may not work perfectly each time, but you can always try again. You can add different pure flavorings, such as mint or lemon. Try a little chocolate or bits of fruit.

Ingredients

½ cup whole milk

1 tablespoon sugar

¼ teaspoon pure vanilla extract
(or other pure flavoring)

Ice cubes

Salt

Equipment

Measuring cups

Measuring spoons

Gallon size ziplock plastic freezer bag

Quart-size ziplock plastic freezer bag

Small bowls for serving

Spoons for eating

Directions

1 Place milk, sugar, and vanilla extract into a quart-size ziplock plastic freezer bag, and then seal it tight.

2 Fill a gallon-size ziplock plastic freezer bag halfway with ice.

3 Put at least 6 tablespoons of salt on top of the ice.

4 Place the quart-size plastic bag inside the gallon-size bag, and seal it tight!

5 Shake and shake and shake. (Note: You might want to wear mittens or gloves while you shake the bags.)

6 The ice cream will become solid in about four minutes or less.

Extension

Explore how salt and ice interact by making ice sculptures!

1. Freeze water in a variety of different-size plastic containers, such as whipped topping tubs, frosting cans, and yogurt cups. Consider adding food coloring to the water before freezing.

2. Take ice out of containers, and place it in a water table or other deep plastic container.

3. Place one part salt to three parts warm water into spray bottles. Set the spray bottles at their stream setting.

4. Spray the ice, and see what effect the salt water has on the ice.

A Book to Read

Curious George Goes to an Ice Cream Shop by Margret Rey and H. A. Rey is a wonderful story about another one of George's adventures.

Yield: Makes 1 serving.

Nutritional information for ice cream: 4 grams fat, 19 grams carbohydrates, 0 grams fiber, 4 grams protein.

Did You Know?

There are over two hundred different types of raspberries in the world. Not all of them are red—there are black and golden varieties, too.

RASPBERRY ORANGE POPS

The combination of raspberries and orange juice is an unexpected treat. Adding evaporated milk to the recipe makes these pops the creamiest ones you'll ever eat.

Ingredients

1 12-ounce can frozen orange juice concentrate
1 12-ounce can evaporated milk
18 ounces of raspberry yogurt
1 tablespoon honey

Equipment

Blender
Measuring spoons
Sharp knife
8-ounce paper cups
Aluminum foil
Craft sticks

Directions

1 In a blender combine ½ can of orange juice concentrate, evaporated milk, yogurt, and honey.

2 Blend for fifteen seconds on high speed. Turn off blender.

3 Pour mixture into cups, filling them halfway.

4 Cover each cup with aluminum foil.

5 With a sharp knife, make a small hole in the center of the foil, and insert a craft stick through the hole into the mixture.

6 Freeze overnight.

7 Remove foil, and remove pops from paper cups to eat.

Extension

What are the differences between concentrated orange juice and premade orange juice?

1. Freeze the remaining orange juice concentrate in ice cube trays.
2. In another ice cube tray freeze premade orange juice.
3. Let the ice cubes set overnight.
4. On the next day break the ice cubes into pieces, and allow the children to taste the different orange ice cubes.
5. List their comments on a chart.
6. With the children, discuss similarities and differences.

A Book to Read

In *Stella and the Berry Thief* by Jane B. Mason, Stella grows the best raspberries in Wisconsin. Her raspberries win many awards, but she does not like to share them. Hear what happens when Stella goes to pick fruit from her raspberry bush only to find the bush empty!

Yield: Makes 9 pops. Serving size 1 pop.
Nutritional information for pops: 3 grams fat, 35 grams carbohydrates, 0 grams fiber, 6 grams protein.

Did You Know?

The Hawaiian alphabet consists of only thirteen characters. A, E, H, I, K, L, M, N, O, P, U, W, and ʻ—the last symbol is called an *okina* and signifies a quick "stop" in the voice.

HAWAIIAN POPS

What a great opportunity to enjoy all the fruits of summer in one pop. A mixture of yogurt and fresh fruit will cool you down on a nice sunny day. Enjoy your pops while wearing a lei.

Ingredients

½ cup pineapple chunks
½ cup sliced bananas
½ cup sliced strawberries
½ cup sliced peaches
2 cups vanilla yogurt

Equipment

Blender
Measuring cups
Sharp knife
Cutting board
8-ounce paper cups
Craft sticks
Aluminum foil

Directions

1 With a sharp knife, cut fruits into bite-size pieces.

2 Place fruit and yogurt in blender. Blend on high speed until well mixed. Turn off blender.

3 Pour mixture into cups, filling them halfway.

4 Cover each cup with aluminum foil.

5 With a sharp knife, make a small hole in the foil, and insert a craft stick through the hole into the mixture.

6 Freeze overnight.

7 Remove foil.

8 Remove pops from paper cups to eat.

Extension

Explore a Hawaiian theme with a craft:

Hibiscus Flowers

1. Fold a coffee filter in half, then in half again, and then in half again.

2. Have children color the coffee filters with washable markers, then drip water on the filter to achieve a "water color" effect for the flowers.

3. Grasp the coffee filter in the middle with two fingers, and twist to make a stem. Add a chenille stick for the longer stem.

4. Hibiscus flowers come in all colors, so go crazy with colors!

A Book to Read

Learn more about the Hawaiian alphabet in the story *A Is for Aloha: A Hawai'i Alphabet* by U'ilani Goldsberry.

Yield: Makes 8 servings. Serving size 1 pop.
Nutritional information for pops: 1 gram fat, 15 grams carbohydrates, 1 gram fiber, 3 grams protein.

FROSTY FRUITY DELIGHT

Pineapple adds a special sweetness to this frosty drink. Its great combination of fruits and fruit juices really hits the spot on a warm day.

Ingredients

2 cups ripe bananas

2 cups orange juice

2 cups 2 percent milk

1 cup canned crushed pineapple, drained

Equipment

Blender

Measuring cups

Sharp knife

Cutting board

Spoons

Clear plastic cups

Plastic wrap

9-by-13-inch pan or plastic container

Directions

1 Cut banana into bite-size pieces.

2 In a blender mix orange juice and milk on high speed.

3 Slowly add banana and pineapple to blender until well mixed. Turn off blender.

4 Pour mixture into a 9-by-13-inch pan, and cover with plastic wrap.

5 Freeze overnight.

6 Scoop mixture into cups, and serve with a spoon.

Extension

Frozen Paper Painting

1. Spray water on any type of paper. The paper should be heavily wet.

2. Place paper in freezer and leave overnight.

3. Using watercolors, paint onto the frozen paper to see what happens!

A Book to Read

A Fruit Is a Suitcase for Seeds by Jean Richards tells the story of where seeds come from and what they will grow into.

Yield: Makes 14 servings. Serving size 1 pop.

Nutritional information for fruit mixture: 1 gram fat, 12 grams carbohydrates, 1 gram fiber, 2 grams protein.

Did You Know?

If you plant a single seed from an orange, you're likely to get more than one plant growing from it.

FROZEN ORANGE BANANA YOGURT POPS

The graham crackers on the bottom of these freezer pops provide a little extra crunch. Add frozen bananas, fruity orange juice, and vanilla yogurt for a frozen drink bursting with flavor!

Ingredients

2 bananas
2 cups orange juice
1 cup vanilla yogurt
2 graham crackers

Equipment

Blender
Sharp knife
Cutting board
Measuring cups
8-ounce clear plastic cups
Aluminum foil
Rolling pin
Craft sticks
Quart-size ziplock plastic storage bag

Directions

1 Cut the bananas into ½-inch pieces.

2 Place orange juice and bananas into the blender. Blend until smooth.

3 Add vanilla yogurt, then blend again until smooth. Turn off blender.

4 Pour mixture into cups, filling them halfway.

5 Place graham crackers in a quart-size ziplock plastic storage bag.

6 Using a rolling pin, crush graham crackers until they become crumbs.

7 Sprinkle graham cracker crumbs on top of yogurt mixture.

8 Cover each cup with aluminum foil.

9 With a sharp knife, make a small hole in the foil, and insert a craft stick through the hole into the mixture.

10 Freeze two to three hours.

11 Remove foil.

12 Remove pops from cups to eat.

Extension

Have an orange feast! Ask families to bring in one food item that is orange. Foods could include oranges, apricots, cheese cubes, carrots, sweet potatoes, and pumpkin.

A Book to Read

Read *Orange: Seeing Orange All around Us* by Sarah L. Schuette to learn more about orange objects through drawings and photographs.

Yield: Makes 8 servings. Serving size 1 pop.
Nutritional information for pops: 1 gram fat, 20 grams carbohydrates, 1 gram fiber, 3 grams protein.

COOKING MEASUREMENT EQUIVALENTS

1 tablespoon	=	3 teaspoons
1⁄16 cup	=	1 tablespoon
⅛ cup	=	2 tablespoons
¼ cup	=	4 tablespoons
⅓ cup	=	5 tablespoons + 1 teaspoon
⅜ cup	=	6 tablespoons
½ cup	=	8 tablespoons
⅔ cup	=	10 tablespoons + 2 teaspoons
¾ cup	=	12 tablespoons
1 cup	=	48 teaspoons
1 cup	=	16 tablespoons
1 cup	=	8 fluid ounces
1 pint	=	2 cups
1 quart	=	2 pints
1 quart	=	4 cups
1 gallon	=	4 quarts
1 pound	=	16 ounces

A GLOSSARY OF COOKING TECHNIQUES

chill: To place in a refrigerator to become cold.

chop: To cut into small bits.

combine: To join ingredients together.

core: To remove the central part of a fruit.

cover: To place a top or lid on an item.

cut: To separate into pieces using a sharp knife.

dice: To cut into small cubes.

divide: To separate into a specific number of servings.

fold: To gently turn the bottom part of food over to the top.

freeze: To put into a freezer to become frozen.

layer: To place food items one on top of another.

mix: To combine.

peel: To remove the skin from a fruit or vegetable.

pour: To make a liquid flow from one container to another.

roll: To move along a surface.

shake: To move up and down to mix ingredients.

slice: To cut a portion of the food.

smash: To squash food into a soft pulp.

spread: To apply a thin layer or coating.

sprinkle: To scatter across a surface.

squeeze: To press together with a hard force.

stir: To mix with a continuous circular motion.

tear: To pull apart.

top: To put on top of the food item.

Appendix C
RECOMMENDED CHILDREN'S BOOKS

Amico, Tom, and James Proimos. 2006. *Raisin and Grape*. New York: Dial Books for Young Readers.

Ancona, George. 2004. *Mi Casa/My House*. New York: Children's Press.

Andreae, Giles, and Vanessa Cabban. 1999. *Love Is a Handful of Honey*. Waukesha, WI: Little Tiger Press.

Bornstein, Ruth. 2000. *Little Gorilla*. New York: Houghton Mifflin.

Braithwaite, Jill. 2004. *From Cane to Sugar*. Minneapolis, MN: Lerner Publications.

Bynum, Janie. 2006. *Nutmeg and Barley: A Budding Friendship*. Cambridge, MA: Candlewick.

Carle, Eric. 1984. *The Mixed-Up Chameleon*. New York: HarperCollins.

———. 1986. *Papa, Please Get the Moon for Me*. Natick, MA: Picture Book Studio.

———. 2000. *The Honeybee and the Robber*. New York: Philomel Books.

———. 2007. *The Very Hungry Caterpillar*. New York: Philomel Books.

Charney, Steve, and David Goldbeck. 2007. *The ABCs of Fruits and Vegetables and Beyond*. Woodstock, NY: Ceres Press.

Christelow, Eileen. 2007. *Five Little Monkeys Go Shopping*. New York: Clarion Books.

Church, Caroline Jayne. 2011. *You Are My Sunshine*. New York: Cartwheel Books.

Coogan, Jim. 2002. *Clarence: The Cranberry Who Couldn't Bounce*. East Dennis, MA: Harvest Home Books.

Dahl, Roald. 2007. *James and the Giant Peach*. New York: Puffin Books.

Ehlert, Lois. 2004. *Pie in the Sky*. New York: Harcourt.

Elliott, George. 2005. *The Boy Who Loved Bananas*. Toronto: Kids Can Press.

French, Vivian. 1998. *Oliver's Fruit Salad*. New York: Orchard Books.

Goldsberry, U'ilani. 2005. *A Is for Aloha: A Hawai'i Alphabet*. Ann Arbor, MI: Sleeping Bear Press.

Hall, Zoe. 1994. *It's Pumpkin Time!* New York: Scholastic.

Harter, Debbie. 2006. *Walking through the Jungle*. Cambridge, MA: Barefoot Books.

Hemingway, Edward. 2012. *Bad Apple: A Tale of Friendship*. New York: Putnam Juvenile.

Hoffman, Mary. 2006. *A First Book of Fairy Tales*. New York: DK Publishing.

Howe, James. 1984. *The Day the Teacher Went Bananas*. New York: Dutton Children's Books.

Johnson, Crockett. 1955. *Harold and the Purple Crayon*. New York: HarperCollins.

Laird, Elizabeth, Roz Davison, and David Sim. 2006. *Jungle School*. New York: Crabtree Publishing.

London, Jonathan. 1995. *Like Butter on Pancakes*. New York: Viking.

Lopez, Mario, Marissa Lopez Wong, and Maryn Roos. 2009. *Mud Tacos!* New York: Celebra Children's Books.

Lottridge, Celia Barker, and Karen Patkau.

2012. *One Watermelon Seed*. Markham, ON: Fitzhenry and Whiteside.

Mahy, Margaret, and Polly Dunbar. 2008. *Bubble Trouble*. New York: Clarion Books.

Maitland, Barbara. 1997. *The Bear Who Didn't Like Honey*. New York: Orchard Books.

Martin, Bill Jr., and John Archambault. 1988. *Up and Down on the Merry-Go-Round*. New York: Henry Holt.

Mason, Jane B. 2004. *Stella and the Berry Thief*. New York: Marshall Cavendish.

McCloskey, Robert. 1948. *Blueberries for Sal*. New York: Viking.

Milne, A. A. 2006. *The Honey Tree*. New York: Golden Books.

Morris, Ann. 1993. *Bread, Bread, Bread*. New York: Harper Collins.

Numeroff, Laura Joffe. 1995. *Chimps Don't Wear Glasses*. New York: Simon and Schuster Books for Young Readers.

Paikai, Tammy. 2009. *Too Many Mangos*. Waipahu, HI: Island Heritage.

Raczka, Bob. 2009. *Summer Wonders*. Morton Grove, IL: Albert Whitman.

Rankin, Laura. 2006. *Fluffy and Baron*. New York: Dial Books for Young Readers.

Rey, Margret, and H. A. Rey. 1989. *Curious George Goes to an Ice Cream Shop*. Boston: Houghton Mifflin.

———. 1998. *Curious George Goes to a Chocolate Factory*. Boston: Houghton Mifflin.

Richards, Jean. 2002. *A Fruit Is a Suitcase for Seeds*. Brookfield, CT: Millbrook Press.

Roth, Susan L. 1998. *Cinnamon's Day Out: A Gerbil Adventure*. New York: Dial Books for Young Readers.

Schuette, Sarah L. 2002. *Orange: Seeing Orange All around Us*. Mankato, MN: Capstone.

———. 2003. *An Alphabet Salad: Fruits and Vegetables from A to Z*. Mankato, MN: Capstone.

Stevens, Janet, and Susan Stevens Crummel. 1999. *Cook-a-Doodle-Do*. Orlando, FL: Harcourt.

Tafuri, Nancy. 2010. *The Busy Little Squirrel*. New York: Simon and Schuster Books for Young Readers.

Vega, Denise. 2008. *Build a Burrito: A Counting Book in English and Spanish*. New York: Scholastic.

Vere, Ed. 2010. *Banana!* New York: Henry Holt.

Wallace, Nancy Elizabeth. 2004. *Apples, Apples, Apples*. New York: Marshall Cavendish.

Waters, Tony. 2003. *Cinnamon's Busy Year*. San Jose, CA: All About Kids Publishing.

Westcott, Nadine Bernard. 1991. *Peanut Butter and Jelly: A Play Rhyme*. Boston: Houghton Mifflin.

Wood, Don, and Audrey Wood. 1993. *The Little Mouse, the Red Ripe Strawberry, and the Big Hungry Bear*. New York: Child's Play International.

INDEX